Imitation is Limitation

BETHANY HOUSE PUBLISHERS
BOOKS BY JOHN MASON

Imitation Is Limitation
The Impossible Is Possible

JOHN MASON

Imitation is Limitation

BETHANYHOUSE
MINNEAPOLIS, MINNESOTA

Published by Bethany House Publishers
11400 Hampshire Avenue South
Bloomington, Minnesota 55438
www.bethanyhouse.com

Bethany House Publishers is a Division of
Baker Book House Company, Grand Rapids, Michigan.

Printed in the United States of America

Library of Congress Cataloging-in-Publication Data

Mason, John, 1955-
    Imitation is limitation : being the unique person God meant you to be / John Mason.
      p. cm.
    ISBN 0-7642-2741-6 (alk. paper)
    1. Self-realization—Religious aspects—Christianity. I. Title.
    BV4598.2.M27   2004
    248.4—dc22   2003023498

JOHN MASON is the founder and president of Insight International, a minister, an inspirational speaker, and the author of ten books, including *An Enemy Called Average*. John, his wife, and their four children live in Tulsa, Oklahoma.

You may contact him with your prayer requests or other inquiries at:

John Mason
Insight International
P.O. Box 54996
Tulsa, OK 74155

www.freshword.com
johnmason@freshword.com

TABLE OF CONTENTS

INTRODUCTION

GOD'S CREATION OF YOU put a smile on His face. Yes, that's what Paul's first letter to the Corinthians tells us. Why, then, do so many people not accept the way God made them? And, even more incredibly, why do they try to change their identity?

God made you *on* purpose *for* a purpose. He has a job for you that no one else can do as well as you. Out of billions of applicants, you're the most qualified.

It's been said that the biggest enemy of great is good. The biggest enemy most of us will face is ourselves, the nagging voice that says, "Be like him; you're not worthy; do what she does; go where the crowd is going." You see, when you're trying to be like someone else, the best you can ever be is second best.

It's time to get our eyes off of others and onto God. People will detour you, but God will always keep you on track. To become the person He intended you to be, use what He has given you. Follow your unique plan: Resist imitation and live the unlimited life.

IF YOU'RE NOT *YOU*, THEN WHO ARE YOU GOING TO BE?

A MIDDLE-AGED WOMAN had a heart attack and was rushed to the emergency room. On the operating table she had a near-death experience; seeing God, she asked if this was it. He said, "No, you have another forty-three years, two months, and eight days to live."

Upon recovery, she decided to stay in the hospital and have a face-lift, liposuction, a tummy tuck, the whole works. She even had someone come in and change her hair color, figuring that since she had so much life remaining, she might as well make the most of it.

She was discharged after the final procedure; however, while crossing the street outside, she was killed by a speeding ambulance.

Arriving in God's presence, she fumed, "I thought you said I had another forty-plus years."

He replied, "I didn't recognize you."

Be yourself. Think about it: Aren't most of the discontented people you know trying to be someone they aren't or trying to do something they're not supposed to do? A Congolese proverb asserts, "Wood may remain ten years in the water, but it will never become a crocodile." Jeremiah asks, "Can the Ethiopian change his skin or the leopard its spots?" (13:23). Julius Hare advised, "Be what you are. This is the first step toward becoming better than you are."

> *The curious paradox is that when I accept myself just as I am, then I can change.*
>
> —CARL ROGERS

Frederic Klopstock remarked, "He who has no opinion of his own, but depends on the opinions of others, is a slave. To only dream of the person you are supposed to be is to waste the person you are." Nobody is as disappointed and unhappy as the person who spends her life longing to be somebody else.

The person who trims himself to suit everybody will soon whittle himself away. If you don't have a plan for your own life, you'll only become a part of someone else's. Never wish to be anything but yourself. Andre Gide counseled, "It is better to be hated for what you are, than loved for what you are not."

> *Until you make peace with who you are, you will never be content with what you have.*
>
> —DORIS MORTMAN

There is only one life for you—your own. The person who walks in someone else's tracks never leaves his own footprints. Most of our challenges in life come from not knowing ourselves and ignoring our true virtues. John Stuart Mill observed, "All good things . . . are the fruit of originality."

Most people live their entire lives as complete strangers to themselves. Don't let that happen to you. Leo Buscaglia admonished,

The easiest thing to be in the world is you. The most difficult thing to be is what other people want you to be. Don't let them put you in that position.

The opposite of courage is not fear but conformity. Nothing in life is more exhausting and frustrating than trying to live it as someone else.

Consider these words from one of history's greatest artists:

My mother said to me, "If you become a soldier you'll become a general; if you become a monk you'll end up as the pope." Instead, I became a painter and wound up as Picasso.

No one ever became great by imitation: Imitation is limitation. Don't be a copy of something. Make your own impression. Dare to be who you are.

ALIBIS LIE

I've missed more than 9,000 shots in my career. I've lost almost 300 games. Twenty-six times I've been trusted to take the game-winning shot . . . and missed. I have failed over and over and over again in my life. And that is why I succeed.

—MICHAEL JORDAN
(ARGUABLY THE GREATEST
BASKETBALL PLAYER EVER)

When it comes to excuses, the world is full of amazing inventors. Don't spend half your life telling what you are going to do and the other half explaining why you didn't do it. An alibi is the supposed proof that you did do what you didn't do, so that others will think you didn't do what you did.

Mistakes have hidden powers to help us, but they fail in their mission of helping us when we blame them on other people. When you use excuses, you give up your power to change and improve. You can fall down many times, but you won't be a failure until you say that someone else pushed you. Edmund

Gosse said, "Never mind whom you praise, but be very careful whom you blame."

If you find an excuse, don't pick it up. Failures are experts at making excuses. There are always enough excuses available if you are weak enough to use them. The world simply does not have enough crutches for all the lame excuses. It's always easier to find excuses than time for the things we don't want to do.

Find a way instead of looking for an alibi. There is no excuse for being full of excuses. When you make a mistake and then make an excuse for it, you have made two mistakes. William Blake noted, "The fox condemns the trap, not himself." Don't find yourself talking like that old fox!

> *Admitting errors clears the score*
> *And proves you wiser than before.*
> —ARTHUR GUITERMAN

Doing a job right is always easier than fabricating an alibi for why you didn't. You waste time and creative energies thinking up excuses.

An excuse is a foundation upon which one builds a house of failure. An alibi is worse and more troubling than a lie, because an alibi is a lie with other lies attached to it. It's been said that an excuse is a thin skin of falsehood stretched tightly over a bald-faced lie.

Most failures come from people who have the habit of making excuses. When you're good at making excuses, it's hard to excel at anything else. Proverbs says, "All hard work brings a profit, but mere talk leads only to poverty" (14:23). Don't make excuses, make progress.

There may be many reasons for failure, but not a single excuse. Never let a challenge become an alibi. You have a choice: Let the obstacle be an alibi, or let it be an opportunity.

No alibi will ever support your purpose in life.

The person who really wants to do something finds a way; the others find an excuse. If you ask a person who has failed in life, you'll be told that success is a matter of luck. Don't buy that alibi.

Don't Build a Case Against Yourself

A BOY AND HIS FATHER are walking in the mountains. Suddenly the son falls, hurts himself, and screams: "AAAhhhhhhhhhhh!!!"

To his surprise, he hears a voice repeating, somewhere on the mountain: "AAAhhhhhhhhhhh!!!"

Curious, he yells: "Who are you?"

He receives the answer: "Who are you?"

Angered at the response, he screams: "Coward!"

He receives the answer: "Coward!"

He looks to his father and asks: "What's going on?"

The father smiles and says: "My son, pay attention."

And then he screams to the mountain: "I admire you!"

The voice answers: "I admire you!"

Again the man screams: "You are a champion!"

The voice retorts: "You are a champion!"

The boy is surprised but does not understand.

Then the father explains: "People call this ECHO, but really, this is LIFE. It gives you back everything you say or do. Our life is simply a reflection of our actions. Life will give you back everything you have given to it" (Anonymous).

Your life is not a coincidence: It's a reflection of you! If you'd like to know who's responsible for the majority of your troubles, take a look in the mirror. If you could kick the person responsible for most of your problems, you wouldn't be able to sit down for three weeks. It's time for us to stay out of our own way.

> *There is little that can withstand a man who can conquer himself.*
>
> —LOUIS XIV

Stewart Johnson commented, "Our business in life is not to get ahead of others, but to get ahead of ourselves—to break our own records, to outstrip our yesterday by our today, to do our work with more force than ever before."

Ralph Waldo Emerson said, "It is impossible for man to be cheated by anyone but himself." Frank Crane noted, "Our best friends and our worst enemies are the thoughts we have about ourselves." Proverbs declares, "As a man thinks within himself, so he is" (23:7). Norman Vincent Peale warned, "Do not build up obstacles in your imagination."

Stop looking only at where you are and start looking at what you can be. Be careful of where your mind wanders; your words and actions follow it.

No one can defeat you unless you first defeat yourself. Self-image sets the boundaries and limitations for each of our individual accomplishments. Charles Caleb Colton said,

> *We are sure to be losers when we quarrel with ourselves; it is civil war.*

If you doubt yourself, listen to Alexandre Dumas: "A person who doubts himself is like a man who enlists in the ranks of his enemy and bears arms against himself." Tim Redmond cautions, "Don't commit treason against your own life and purpose."

You carry with you the world in which you must live. Know this: When you have a great dream, your mind will be your biggest foe. Huge obstacles in your life? James Allen answered, "You are the handicap you must face. You are the one who must choose your place." Remember: You are your own doctor when it comes to curing cold feet, a hot head, and a stuffy attitude.

Frank Tyger says, "Your future depends on many things, but mostly on you." You may succeed if nobody else believes in you, but you will never succeed if you don't believe in yourself. Zig Ziglar observes, "What you picture in your mind, your mind will go to work to accomplish. When you change your pictures, you automatically change your performance." Whatever you attach consistently to the words "I am," you will become.

Enthusiasm Takes You Where Talent Alone Can't

YOU CAN'T DELIVER the goods if your heart is heavier than the load.

We act as though comfort and luxury were the chief requirements of life, when all that we need to make us really happy is something to be enthusiastic about.
—CHARLES KINGSLEY

One of the easiest ways to do this is to count your blessings; do this instead of thinking that your blessings don't count.

Think excitement, talk excitement, act out excitement, and you will become an excited person. Life will take on a new zest, with deeper interests and greater meaning. You can talk, think, and act yourself into enthusiasm or dullness and into monotony or into unhappiness. By the same process you can build up inspiration, excitement, and a surging depth of joy.
—NORMAN VINCENT PEALE

You can succeed at almost anything for which you have

limitless enthusiasm. The world belongs to the enthusiastic.

Your enthusiasm reflects your reserves, your unexploited resources, and perhaps your future output. Winston Churchill said, "Success is going from failure to failure without loss of enthusiasm." You will never rise to great heights without joy and zeal.

Papyrus reminded us, "No one keeps up his enthusiasm automatically." Enthusiasm must be nourished with new actions, new aspirations, new efforts, and new vision. It's your own fault if your enthusiasm is gone: You have failed to feed it. What's enthusiasm? Henry Chester answered, "Nothing more or less than faith in action." Helen Keller said,

Optimism is the faith that leads to achievement.

Nothing we do gets accomplished without hope or confidence.

It isn't our *position* but our *disposition* that makes us happy. Some people freeze in the winter; others ski. A positive attitude always creates positive results. Attitude is a little thing that makes a big difference. Depression, gloom, pessimism, despair, and discouragement stop more people than all illnesses combined.

If you live a life of negativity, you will find yourself seasick during your entire voyage. The negative person is half-defeated before even beginning. I agree with Winston Churchill: "I am an optimist. It does not seem too much use being anything else." Have you ever noticed that no matter how many worries a pessimist has, he always has room for one more? Remember the Chinese proverb: "It is better to light a candle than to curse the darkness." Das Energi said, "Vote with your life. Vote yes!"

There is a direct correlation between our passion and our potential. If you're the light of the world, no one will know it unless the switch is turned on. Follow the directive of Ecclesiastes: "Whatever your hand finds to do, do it with all your might" (9:10). Being positive is essential to achievement and the foundation of true progress.

THOMAS EDISON WAS AFRAID OF THE DARK

Y ES! EDISON WAS AFRAID of the dark—yet he overcame that obstacle in a big way and invented the light bulb.

Times of general calamity and confusion have ever been productive of the greatest minds. The purest ore is produced from the hottest furnace, and the brightest thunderbolt is the one elicited from the darkest storm.

—CHARLES CALEB COLTON

The door to opportunity swings on the hinges of adversity. Problems are the price of progress. The obstacles of life are intended to make us better, not bitter. Adversity has advantages.

Alfred D. Souza said,

For a long time it had seemed to me that life was about to begin—REAL LIFE. But there was always some obstacle in the way, something to be gotten through first, some unfinished business, time still to be served, and a debt to be paid. Then, life would begin. At last it dawned on me that these obstacles were my life.

Obstacles are merely a call to strengthen, not quit. Ann Gimenez says, "Between you and anything significant will be giants in your path." You cannot bring about change without confrontation. The truth is, if you like things easy, you will have difficulties. If you like problems, you will succeed. The biggest successes are the people who solve the biggest problems.

If you have a dream without problems, you don't really have a dream. Have the attitude of Louisa May Alcott: "I am not afraid of storms, for I am learning how to sail my ship."

Circumstances are the rulers of the weak; but they are the instruments of the wise.

—SAMUEL GLOVER

Don't let your problems take the lead—*you* take it. The difficulty you face is simply an opportunity for you to do your best.

The Chinese have a maxim that says, "The gem cannot be polished without friction, nor man perfected without trials." It seems that hardship is the necessary preparation for greatness. Consider what Jesus said: "Here on earth you will have many trials and sorrows; but cheer up, for I have overcome the world."

What attitude do we need to have toward difficulties? William Boetcker said, "The difficulties and struggles of today are but the best price we must pay for the accomplishment and victory of tomorrow." Lou Holtz advised, "Adversity is another way to measure the greatness of individuals. I never had a crisis that didn't make me stronger."

When you encounter obstacles, you will discover things about yourself that you never knew. You will also find out what you really believe. Every problem introduces a person to himself.

Challenges make you stretch—they make you go beyond the norm. Turning an obstacle to your advantage is the first step toward victory.

The ultimate measure of man is not where he stands in moments of comfort and convenience, but where he stands at times of challenge and controversy.
—MARTIN LUTHER KING JR.

Life is as uncertain as a grapefruit's squirt. Sydney Harris mused, "When I hear somebody say that 'Life is hard,' I am always tempted to ask, 'Compared to what?'" We might as well face our problems; we can't run fast or far enough to get away from them all. We should have the attitude of Hall-of-Famer Stan Musial: Commenting on how to handle a spitter, he said, "I'll just hit the dry side of the ball." Charles Kettering said, "No one would have crossed the ocean if he could have gotten off the ship in the storm." The breakfast of champions is not cereal; it's obstacles.

HONESTY IS STILL THE BEST POLICY

THE TRUTH OUTLIVES A LIE.

A clergyman was walking down the street when he came upon a dozen boys, all of them apparently between ten and twelve years of age.

They were surrounding a dog. Concerned, he went over and asked, "What are you doing with that dog?"

One of the boys replied, "He's an old neighborhood stray. We all want him, but only one of us can take him home. So we've decided that whichever one of us can tell the biggest lie will get to keep the dog."

Of course the reverend was taken aback. "You boys shouldn't be having a contest telling lies!" he exclaimed. He then launched into a ten-minute sermon beginning with, "Don't you boys know it's a sin to lie?" and ending with, "Why, when I was your age, I never told a lie."

There was dead silence for about a minute. Just as the reverend was beginning to think he'd gotten through to them, the smallest boy gave a deep sigh and said, "All right, give him the dog."

There is no limit to the height you can attain by remaining

on the level. Even though honesty is still the best policy, today it seems there are fewer policyholders than there used to be. George Braque said, "Truth exists; only falsehood has to be invented." Miguel de Cervantes said, "Truth will rise above falsehood as oil above water."

White lies leave black marks on your reputation. You can't stretch the truth without making your story look pretty thin, and when you stretch the truth, it snaps back at you.

Truth will win every argument if you stick with it long enough. Though honesty may not be popular, it is always right. The fact that nobody wants to believe what's true doesn't prevent it from being correct.

Two half-truths don't make a whole truth. In fact, beware of half-truths: You may have gotten hold of the wrong half. You will find that a lie has no legs; it has to be supported by other lies. T. L. Osborn advises,

> *Always tell the truth, and you never have to remember what you said.*

The truth is one thing for which there is no known substitute. There is no acceptable replacement for honesty; there is no valid excuse for dishonesty, and nothing shows dirt like a white lie. It may seem that a lie has taken care of the present, but it has no future. Hope built on a lie is always the beginning of loss—a shady person never produces a bright life.

Herbert Casson promised, "Show me a liar, and I will show you a thief." A lie's main assignment is to steal from you and from others. George Bernard Shaw said,

> *The liar's punishment is not in the least that he is not believed, but that he cannot believe anyone else.*

Liars have no true friends, for how can you trust them?

> *If you lie and then tell the truth, the truth will be considered a lie.*
>
> —SUMERIAN PROVERB

That is, a liar will not be believed even if he tells the truth. An honest person alters his ideas to fit the truth; a dishonest person alters the truth to fit his ideas.

There are no degrees of honesty. The only way to be free is to be a person of truth. Truth is strong, and it *will* prevail— there is no power on earth more overpowering than the truth. Consider the words of Pearl Buck: "Truth is always exciting. Speak it, then. Life is dull without it."

PERSISTENCE PREVAILS
WHEN ALL ELSE FAILS

A MAN WHO MEETS A GURU on the road asks, "Which way is success?"

The bearded sage doesn't speak but instead points to a place off in the distance.

The man, thrilled by the prospect of quick and easy success, rushes off in the appropriate direction. *Splat!*

He limps back, bruised and stunned, assuming he must have misinterpreted the message. He repeats his question to the guru, who again points silently in the same direction.

He obediently walks off once more. This time the splat is deafening, and when he crawls back, he is bloody, broken, and irate. "I asked you which way is success!" he screams at the guru. "I followed the direction you indicated! And all I got was splattered! No more of this pointing! Talk!"

Only then does the guru speak: "Success *is* that way. Just a little after the splat."

All of us have experienced "the splat." It's what we do *after* the splat that makes all the difference. Many times this is what separates high achievers from non-achievers. *Whatever you want to accomplish in life will require persistence*. Champion racer Rick Mears said it well: "To finish first you must first finish."

Do you want to accomplish something in life? Be like the stone cutter.

> *Look at the stone cutter, hammering away at the rock, perhaps a hundred times without as much as a crack showing in it. Yet at the hundred and first blow it will split in two, and I know it was not the last blow that did it, but all that had gone before.*
>
> —JACOB RIIS

All things come to those who persistently go after them. Perseverance is the result of a strong will; stubbornness is the result of a strong won't. Baron de Montesquieu said, "Success often depends on knowing how long it will take to succeed." This is the secret of success: Never let down, and never let up. Consider what Proverbs says: "Seest thou a man diligent in his business? he shall stand before kings" (22:29 KJV).

> *You may be whatever you resolve to be. Determine to be something in the world and you will be something. "I cannot" never accomplished anything; "I will try" has wrought wonders.*
>
> —JOEL HAUSE

Herbert Kaufman adds, "Spurts don't count. The final score makes no mention of a splendid start if the finish proves that you were an 'also ran.'"

Keep in mind the words of Hamilton Holt: "Nothing worthwhile comes easily. Half effort does not produce half results. It produces no results. Work, continuous work and hard work, is the only way to accomplish results that last."

No one *finds* life worth living. You must *make* it worth living.

Ralph Waldo Emerson said, "The great majority of men are bundles of beginnings." I agree with Charles Kettering: "Keep on going and the chances are you will stumble on something perhaps when you are least expecting it." Be like Winston Churchill's bulldog:

> *The nose of the bulldog is slanted backwards so he can continue to breathe without letting go.*

The truth is that persistence can be a bitter plant, but it has sweet fruit. Joseph Ross said, "It takes time to succeed because success is merely the natural reward of taking time to do anything well." Victory always comes to the most persevering.

Persistent people begin their success where most others quit. Many times success consists of hanging on one minute longer. Calvin Coolidge said, "'Press on' has solved and always will solve the problems of the human race." You will find that persistent people always have this attitude: they never lose the game; they just run out of time.

Hold on; hold fast; hold out. Patience is genius.
—GEORGES-LOUIS LECLERC,
COMPTE DE BUFFON

DESTINY DRAWS

ARE YOU STUMBLING TOWARD an uncertain future? You can predict your future by the awareness you have of your unique purpose. Too many people know what they are running from but not what they are running to. First, concentrate on finding your purpose, then concentrate on fulfilling it. Having a powerful *why* will provide you with the necessary *how*. Purpose, not money or talent, can be your strongest asset.

Myles Monroe said, "There is something for you to start that is destined for you to finish." Take care of your purpose, and the end will take care of itself. When you base your life on principle, 99 percent of your decisions are already made. Considering an action? Listen to Marcus Aurelius: "Without a purpose nothing should be done."

> *The height of your accomplishments will equal the depth of your convictions. Seek happiness for its own sake, and you will not find it; seek for purpose, and happiness will follow as a shadow comes with the sunshine.*
>
> —WILLIAM SCOLAVINO

As you reach for your destiny, it will be like a magnet that pulls you, not like a brass ring that goes around only once. *Destiny draws.*

John Foster said, "It is a poor, disgraceful thing not to be able to reply, with some degree of certainty, to the simple questions, 'What will you be? What will you do?'" Charles Garfield adds, "Peak performers are people who are committed to a compelling mission. It is very clear that they care deeply about what they do and their efforts, energies and enthusiasms are traceable back to that particular mission." *You're not truly free until you've been made captive by your mission in life.*

William Cowper observed,

> *The only true happiness comes from squandering ourselves for a purpose.*

Proverbs counsels, "Whatever your plan is, just know that nothing else will satisfy you." I agree with Robert Byrne: "The purpose of life is a life of purpose."

Don't part company with your future—it is an anchor in the storm. A purposeless life is an early death. What you believe about your mission in life is the force that determines what you accomplish or fail to accomplish during your time on earth.

The average person's life consists of twenty years of having their parents ask where he or she is going, a few decades of having a spouse ask the same question, and at the end, the mourners wondering the same thing. Martin Luther King Jr. said, "If a man hasn't discovered something that he will die for, he isn't fit to live." Abandon yourself to destiny.

YOU CAN ONLY LIVE TODAY

SEIZE THE MOMENT! Opportunities are constantly either coming *to you* or *by you*. Today was once the future from which you expected so much in the past. Horatio Dresser said, "The ideal never comes. Today is ideal for him who makes it so." Live for today. Don't let what you have within your grasp today be lost entirely because the future intrigues you and the past disheartens you.

Doing your best at this moment puts you in the best place for the next moment. When can you live if not now? All the flowers of tomorrow are in the seeds of today. Seneca said, "Begin at once to live." Ellen Metcalf remarked, "There are many people who are at the right place at the right time but don't know it." It is okay to take time to plan, but when the time of action has arrived, stop thinking and go for it!

Marie Edgeworth declared,

There is no moment like the present. The man who will not execute his resolutions when they are fresh on him can have no hope from them afterwards; for they will be dissipated, lost, and perished in the hurry and scurry of the world, or sunk in the slough of indolence.

John Burroughs urged,

*The lesson which life repeats and constantly reinforces
is, "Look underfoot." You are always nearer than you
think. . . . The great opportunity is where you are. Do
not despise your own place and hour.*

The most important thing in our lives is what we are doing
now: "This is the day that the Lord has made, I will rejoice and
be glad in it."

Don't ever start your day in neutral. Know the real value of
today. Make real the words of Jonathan Swift: "May you live all
the days of your life." The future that you long and dream for
begins today. Ralph Waldo Emerson said, "Write it on your
heart that every day is the best day of the year."

Most people's "life regrets" come from failing to act when
they have an opportunity. Albert Dunning said, "Great opportunities come to all, but many do not know that they have met
them. The only preparation to take advantage of them is to
watch what each day brings."

Noah didn't wait for his ship to come in—he built one. Few
know when to rise to the occasion; most only know when to
sit down. Many spend too much time dreaming of what's coming, never realizing that a little of it arrives every day. Ruth
Schabacker nails it:

*Every day comes bearing its own gifts. Untie the
ribbons.*

Martial warned, "Tomorrow, life is too late; live today."
Wayne Dyer observes, "Now is all we have. Everything that has
ever happened, anything that is ever going to happen to you, is
just a thought." Today, well lived, will prepare you for both the
opportunities and obstacles of tomorrow.

BE A LITTLE KINDER THAN YOU HAVE TO BE

SERVING OTHERS IS ONE of life's most awesome privileges. Albert Schweitzer said, "The only ones among you who will really be happy are those who have sought and found how to serve." Pierre Teilhard de Chardin commented, "The most satisfying thing in life is to have been able to give a large part of oneself to others." Follow the counsel of Carl Reilland:

In about the same degree as you are helpful you will be happy.

Hunt for the good points in people. Remember, they have to do the same in your case. Then do something to help them. If you want to get ahead, be a bridge instead of a wall. Love others more than they deserve. Frank Crane said, "The Golden Rule is of no use unless you realize that it is your move." Each human being presents us with an opportunity to serve. Everybody needs help from somebody.

The entire population of the universe, with one trifling exception, is composed of others.

—JOHN ANDREW HOLMES

Too often we expect everyone else to practice the Golden Rule. The Golden Rule may be old, but it hasn't been used enough to show any signs of wear. We make a first-class mistake if we treat others as second-class people.

You can't help others without helping yourself. Kindness is one of the most difficult things to give away, since it usually comes back to you. The person who sows seeds of kindness enjoys a perpetual harvest. Henry Drummond mused, "I wonder why it is that we are not kinder to each other . . . how much the world needs it! How easily it is done!"

Do you want to get along better with others? Be a little kinder than necessary. A good way to forget your own troubles is to help others out of theirs. When you share, you increase rather than lessen your life.

Theodore Spear said, "You can never expect too much of yourself in the matter of giving yourself to others." The taller a bamboo grows, the lower it bends. True leadership begins with servanthood.

> *One of the most amazing things ever said on earth is Jesus' statement, "He that is greatest among you shall be your servant." None have one chance in a billion of being thought of as really great a century after they're gone except those who have been servants of all.*
>
> —HARRY EMERSON FOSDICK

Henry Burton wrote:

> *Have you had a kindness shown?*
> *Pass it on.*
> *'Twas not given for thee alone,*
> *Pass it on.*

Let it travel down the years,
Let it wipe another's tears,
Till in heaven the deed appears—
Pass it on.

A Parking Meter Reminds Us That We Lose Money Standing Still

—Bert Krose

SUCCESS COMES FROM DARING to take small steps. After being faithful in small steps, you'll look back and be able to say, "I'm still not where I want to be, but I'm not where I was." Julia Carney said,

Little drops of water, little grains of sand,
Make the mighty ocean and the pleasant land.

Louis L'Amour wrote, "Victory is won not in miles but in inches. Win a little now, hold your ground, and later win a lot more." Sometimes we're given a little in order to see what we will do with a lot.

Dale Carnegie said, "Don't be afraid to give your best to what seemingly are small jobs. Every time you conquer one it makes you that much stronger. If you do the little jobs well, the big ones will tend to take care of themselves." Your future comes one hour at a time. Thomas Huxley observed,

The rung of a ladder was never meant to rest upon, but to enable a man to put his other foot higher.

Are you willing to do something *small* for God? Small steps are a big idea. Never be discouraged when you make progress, no matter how slow or small. Only be wary of standing still. Successes are persons who do what they can with what they have, and who do it where they are. Helen Keller said, "I long to accomplish a great and noble task, but it is my chief duty to accomplish small tasks as if they were great and noble."

Nobody makes the greater mistake than he who did nothing because he could only do a little.

—EDMUND BURKE

Small deeds done are better than great deeds planned. I believe that we should care just as much about the small things in our lives as the big things. Why? If we are faithful in the small things, the big things will take care of themselves.

The prize of successfully completing one duty is the opportunity to do another. Robert Smith said, "Most of the critical things in life, which become the starting points of human destiny, are little things." Do little things now, and big things will come to you asking to be done.

One thing is certain: What isn't tried won't work. The most important thing is to begin, even though the first step is the hardest. I agree with Vince Lombardi: "Inches make champions." Take one small step right now. Don't ignore the small things. The kite flies because of its tail. It's the little things that count: Sometimes a safety pin carries more responsibility than a bank president.

David Storey remarked, "Have confidence that if you have done a *little* thing well, you could do a *bigger* thing well, too."

Consider what Pat Robertson said: "Despise not the day of small beginnings because you can make all your mistakes anonymously." Value the little things. One day you may look back and realize they were the big things. Dante Alighieri said, "From a little spark may burst a mighty flame."

> *Remember this on your way up:*
> *The biggest dog was once a pup.*
> —ANONYMOUS

Do Something

J IMMY'S MOTHER CALLED OUT to him at seven in the morning, "Jimmy, get up! It's time for school." There was no answer. She called again, this time more loudly, "Jimmy, get up! It's time for school." Once more there was no answer. Exasperated, she went to his room and shook him, saying, "Jimmy, it's time to get ready for school."

He answered, "Mother, I'm not going to school. There are fifteen hundred kids at that school and every one of them hates me. I'm not going to school."

"Go to school!" she replied sharply.

"But, Mother, all the teachers hate me too. I saw three of them talking the other day and one of them was pointing his finger at me. I know they all hate me, so I'm not going to school," Jimmy answered.

"Go to school!" his mother demanded again.

"But, Mother, I don't understand it. Why would you want to put me through all that torture and suffering?" he protested.

"Jimmy, for two good reasons," she fired back. "First, you're forty-two years old. Second, you're the principal."

There are few of us who, on some days, have not felt like

Jimmy. We just don't want to go to school. That school, of course, is life itself, where dropping out or playing hooky can seem a much better idea than facing the challenges that inevitably lie ahead. Success begins the moment we understand that life is about *beginning*.

Start where you are. You can only start with what you have, not with what you don't have. Opportunity is always where you are, never where you were. To get anywhere, you must launch out for somewhere or you will get nowhere.

Hamilton Mabie said, "The question for each man to settle is not what he would do if he had the means, time, influence, and educational advantages, but what he will do with the things he has." Each of us has an ability to begin to create what we need from something that is already here.

We tend to underrate or overrate what we don't possess. Ed Howe said, "People are always neglecting something they can do and trying to do something they can't do."

Follow the lead of Teddy Roosevelt:

Do what you can, with what you have, where you are.

The only way to learn anything thoroughly is by starting at the bottom (except when learning how to swim). To be successful, do what you can.

Ken Keys Jr. said, "To be upset over what you don't have is to waste what you do have." The truth is that many are successful because they didn't have the advantages others had.

Epicurus said, "Do not spoil what you have by desiring what you have not; but remember that what you now have was once among the things only hoped for." Henri Frederic Amiel observed,

Almost everything comes from almost nothing.

No improvement is as certain as that which proceeds from the right and timely use of what you already have. All those who arrive had to begin where they were.

The truth is, you can't know what you can do until you try. The most important catalyst to reaching your dream is starting right where you are. Edward Everett Hail said, "I cannot do everything, but I can do something. And I will not let what I cannot do interfere with what I can do."

No longer forward nor behind
I look in hope or fear;
But, grateful, take the good I find,
The best of now and here.
                                    —JOHN GREENLEAF WHITTIER

Don't Stop Faster
Than You Start

BRINGING A GIRAFFE into the world is a tall order. A baby giraffe falls ten feet from its mother's womb and usually lands on its back. Within seconds it rolls over and tucks its legs under its body. From this position it considers the world for the first time and shakes off the last vestiges of the birthing fluid from its eyes and ears. Then the mother giraffe rudely introduces its offspring to the reality of life.

In his book *A View From the Zoo*, Gary Richmond describes how a newborn giraffe learns its first lesson.

The mother giraffe lowers her head long enough to take a quick look. Then she positions herself directly over her calf. She waits for about a minute, and then she does the most unreasonable thing: She swings her long, pendulous leg outward and kicks her baby, sending it sprawling head over heels.

When it doesn't get up, the violent process is repeated over and over again. The struggle to rise is momentous. As the baby calf grows tired, the mother kicks it again to stimulate its efforts. Finally, the calf stands for the first time on its wobbly legs.

Then the mother giraffe does something remarkable. She

kicks it off its feet again. Why? She wants it to remember how it got up. In the wild, baby giraffes must be able to get up as quickly as possible to stay with the herd, where there is safety. Lions, hyenas, leopards, and hunting dogs all enjoy young (isolated) giraffes, and if the mother didn't teach her calf to get up quickly and get with it, it'd be easy prey.

There's a common thread that runs through the lives of exceptional people. They are beaten over the head, knocked down, vilified, and for years they get nowhere. But every time they're knocked down they stand up. You cannot destroy these people.

The world will always give you the opportunity to quit, but only the world would call quitting an opportunity.

—CLINT BROWN

As an author, I have the privilege of signing many books. I like to write encouraging expressions in each book before I sign my name. One of the most common sayings I write is *Never give up!* This simple statement is one of the most powerful success principles ever preached.

Joel Budd remarked, "It isn't the final say so, unless *you* say so." Richard Nixon mused,

A man is not finished when he is defeated. He is finished when he quits.

Nobody and nothing can keep you down unless you decide not to rise again. H. E. Jansen said, "The man who wins may have been counted out several times, but he didn't hear the referee." Find a way to, not a way *not* to.

A lazy man is always judged by what he doesn't do. The choice of giving up or going on is a defining moment in your life. You cannot turn back the clock. But you can wind it up again.

A couple of years ago I had the privilege of meeting Peter Lowe, the founder of the successful *Success Seminars*. As we talked, he commented, "The most common trait I have found in all people that are successful is that they have conquered the temptation to give up." One of the best ways to give your best a chance is to rise up when you're knocked down.

In trying times, don't stop trying. Instead of stopping, follow this English proverb: "Don't fall before you are pushed." Margaret Thatcher understood the principle of persistence:

You may have to fight a battle more than once to win it.

David Zucker added, "Quit now, you'll never make it. If you disregard this advice you'll be halfway there."

"I can't!" is the conclusion of fools. Listen to Clare Booth Luce:

There are no hopeless situations, there are only men who have grown hopeless about them.

Admiral Chester Nimitz prayed, "God, grant me the courage not to give up what I think is right even though I think it is hopeless." Giving up is the ultimate tragedy. Archie Moore, the famous boxer, reflected, "If I don't get off the mat, I'll lose the fight."

The choice is simple. *You can either stand up and be counted, or lie down and be counted out.* Defeat never comes to people until they admit it. Your success will be measured by your willingness to keep on trying. Anyone can quit. Have the courage to live.

You Can't Stop a Pig From Wallowing in the Mud

—Yorba

M Y FRIEND NEIL ESKELIN tells a story about a man who died and met Saint Peter at the pearly gates. Realizing that the apostle was wise and knowledgeable, he said, "Saint Peter, I have been interested in military history for many years. Tell me—who was the greatest general of all time?"

Saint Peter quickly responded, "Oh, that's a simple question." He pointed. "It's that man right over there."

The man said, "You must be mistaken. I knew that man on earth. He was just a common laborer."

"That's right, my friend," replied Saint Peter. "But he would have been the greatest general of all time—if he had been a general."

You were created with natural abilities and an internal compass that guides you toward a particular focus for your life. That's only the starting point; the next step is yours. You have an obligation to expand that potential to its ultimate destiny.

Michelangelo said, "It is only well with me when I have a chisel in my hand."

Discover what you are supposed to do, and do it!

I have the opportunity to spend large segments of time in airports because I travel frequently. Almost invariably, I notice scores of people who look like they are in a hurry to nowhere. Isn't it incredible that so many people devote their whole lives to fields of endeavor that have nothing to do with the gifts and talents inside them? Incredibly, many actually spend their entire lives trying to change the way they were made.

Every person has specific gifts, talents, and strengths. Paul told the Corinthians that *every* person has his own gift from God. Marcus Aurelius said, "Take full account of the excellencies which you possess and in gratitude remember how you would hanker after them if you had them not."

Robert Quillen reflected,

> *If you count all your assets you'll always show a profit.*

Seize opportunities to use your gifts: "Put yourself on view. This always brings your talents to light" (Balthasar Gracian). Never judge yourself by your weaknesses. I agree with Malcolm Forbes: "Too many people overvalue what they are not and undervalue what they are." You are richer than you think you are.

Nathaniel Emmons said, "One principal reason why men are so often useless is that they neglect their own profession or calling and divide and shift their attention among a multitude of objects and pursuits." Your best will always arise when you tap into the best gifts inside you.

> *One well cultivated talent, deepened and enlarged, is worth one hundred shallow faculties.*
>
> —WILLIAM MATTHEWS

Too many people take only their wants into consideration, neglecting their talents and abilities. Deep down inside, if you are a musician, then make music. If you are a teacher, teach. Be what you are, and you will be at peace with yourself. I agree with William Boetecher: "The more you learn what to do with yourself, and the more you do for others, the more you will learn to enjoy the abundant life." Do what's most natural for you.

> *To be nobody but yourself—in a world that is doing its best, night and day, to make you everybody else— means to fight the hardest battle that any human being can fight and never stop fighting.*
>
> —E. E. CUMMINGS

The bottom line: Be yourself!

Consider the words of Sydney Harris: "Ninety percent of the world's woe comes from people not knowing themselves, their abilities, their frailties, and even their real virtues." Don't expect anything original from an echo. Alfred de Musset said, "How glorious it is—and also how painful—to be an exception." Billy Walder adds,

> *Trust your own instincts. Your mistakes might as well be your own, instead of someone else's.*

Abraham Lincoln said it best: "Whatever you are, be a good one." Be yourself, then—who else is better qualified?

People Don't Fail So Much As Give Up Easily

THERE WERE TWO MEN SHIPWRECKED on an island. The minute they got onto the island one of them started screaming and yelling, "We're going to die! We're going to die! There's no food! No water! We're going to die!"

The second man was propped up against a palm tree and acting so calmly it drove the first man crazy.

"Don't you understand?!? We're going to die!!"

The second man replied, "You don't understand; I make $100,000 a week."

The first man, dumbfounded, looked at him and asked, "What difference does that make? We're on an island with no food and no water—we're going to DIE!!!"

The second man answered, "I make $100,000 a week, and I tithe ten percent. My pastor will find me."

When you are persistent, you know it, and so does everyone else.

Never give up on what you really know you should do. Failure is waiting on the path of least persistence. The "man of the hour" spent many days and nights getting there: "My overnight success was the longest night of my life" (Unknown). Winners simply do what losers don't want to do . . . longer.

The famous old saying is true:

In the confrontation between the stream and the rock, the stream always wins—not through strength but through perseverance.

Christopher Morley said, "Big shots are only little shots that keep shooting." Persistence is simply enjoying the distance between the birth and the fulfillment of your dreams. An "overnight success" takes years.

We should be people of strong *will*s, not strong *won't*s. Many of the world's great failures did not realize how close they were to success when they gave up. Stopping at third base adds no more to the score than striking out.

Persistence is proof you have not been defeated. Mike Murdock says, "You have no right to anything you have not pursued, for the proof of desire is in the pursuit." Life holds no greater wealth than that of steadfast commitment. You cannot be robbed of it; you can lose it only by your will.

When faithfulness is most difficult, it is most necessary, because trying times are no time to quit trying. The secret of success is to start from scratch and keep on scratching. We rate success by what people finish, not by what they start.

Earl Nightingale said,

A young man once asked a great and famous older man, "How can I make a name for myself in the world and become successful?" The great and famous man replied: "You have only to decide upon what it is you want and then stay with it, never deviating from your course no matter how long it takes, or how rough the road, until you have accomplished it."

Success is found by holding on long after others have let go.

You Have the Potential and Opportunity for Success

D_{O YOU KNOW WHAT THIS PAGE is noted for? From this page you can go anywhere you want to. This page can be the springboard to your future. You can start here and begin to move forward.}

> *Eli Whitney was laughed at when he showed his cotton gin. [Thomas] Edison had to install his electric light free of charge in an office building before anyone would even look at it. The first sewing machine was smashed to pieces by a Boston mob. People scoffed at the idea of railroads. People thought that traveling thirty miles an hour [in an automobile] would stop the circulation of the blood. [Samuel] Morse had to plead before ten Congresses before they would even look at his telegraph.*
>
> —ANONYMOUS

Yet for all these men the sky was not the limit.

Beware of those who stand aloof and greet each venture with reproof; the world would stop if things were run by men who say, "It can't be done."

—SAMUEL GLOVER

We achieve in proportion to what we attempt. However, more people are persuaded into believing in nothing than into believing too much. The truth is that you are never as far from the answer as it first appears.

Each of us has the potential and opportunity for success. It takes just as much effort to lead an unproductive life as it does an effective life, and it always costs more not to do what's right than to do it. Still, millions lead aimless lives in prisons of their own making—simply because they haven't decided how to invest.

Lots of folks confuse bad management [decision-making] with destiny.

—KIN HUBBARD

"Where there is no vision, the people perish," says the book of Proverbs (29:18 KJV). It's not the absence of things that makes you unhappy—it's the absence of vision.

You can predict a person's future by her awareness of her destiny. Life's heaviest burden is to have nothing to carry. The impact of any person is determined by the cause for which he lives and the price he is willing to pay. What you set your heart on will determine how you spend your life.

Do not take lightly your dreams and hopes. Cherish them, for they are like children birthed within you. "It is better to die for something than it is to live for nothing," says Bob Jones Sr. A man without principle never draws much interest.

No wind blows in favor of a ship without a destination. A

person without a goal is like a ship without a rudder. It is not the man with a motive but the man with a purpose who prevails: "Every man's destiny is his life preserver" (*The Sunday School*).

God plants no yearning in the human soul that He does not have a plan to satisfy. Jesus is a man of purpose: "To this end was I born, and for this cause came I into the world, that I should bear witness unto the truth" (John 18:37 KJV). Unfortunately, "we distrust our heart too much, and our head not enough" (Joseph Roux).

A lot of people no longer hope for the best; they just hope to avoid the worst. Too many have heard opportunity knocking at their door, but by the time they unhooked the chain, pushed back the bolt, turned two locks, and shut off the burglar alarm—it was gone!

People generally have myriad opinions and few convictions. A person going nowhere can be sure of reaching his destination. Again: Life's heaviest burden is to have nothing to carry.

You Grow to the Extent That You Give Out

OVER ONE HUNDRED YEARS AGO a woman, wearing a faded gingham dress, and her husband, dressed in a threadbare suit, stepped off the train in Boston and walked timidly into the outer office of the Harvard University president. The secretary instantly decided that these backwoods country hicks had no business at Harvard. She frowned.

"We want to see the president," the man said softly.

"He'll be busy all day," the secretary snapped.

"We'll wait," the woman replied.

For hours the secretary ignored them, hoping they'd become discouraged and go away. They didn't. The secretary gradually grew frustrated, and finally she decided to disturb the president: "Maybe if you just see them for a few minutes, they'll leave," she told him. He sighed in exasperation and agreed.

The president, stern-faced and haughty, strutted toward the couple. The woman began to speak: "We had a son that attended Harvard for one year. He loved Harvard and was happy here. About a year ago, he was accidentally killed. My husband and I would like to erect a memorial to him somewhere on campus."

The president wasn't touched. "Madam," he said condescendingly, "we can't put up a statue for every person who attended Harvard and then died. If we did, this place would look like a cemetery."

"Oh, no," she explained quickly. "We don't want to erect a statue. We thought we would like to give a building to Harvard."

The president rolled his eyes. He glanced at the gingham dress and threadbare suit, then exclaimed: "A building! Do you have any earthly idea how much a building costs? We have over seven and a half million dollars in the buildings at Harvard."

For a moment she was silent. The president was pleased—he could get rid of them now. But she turned to her husband and said, "Is that all it costs to start a university? Why don't we start our own?" Her husband nodded, and they left.

The president's face clouded in confusion and bewilderment; Mr. and Mrs. Leland Stanford walked away and eventually traveled to Palo Alto, California, where they established the university that bears their name—a memorial to a son that Harvard no longer cared about.

The president of Harvard and his secretary judged the Stanfords by their "covering" and missed the opportunity for an enormous endowment. This story (though we cannot verify its validity) points out how important it is to see people as God sees them and not to judge them by what they wear, where they live, what they drive, or how they speak. It really is God's idea to care for people regardless of what they can give or how they appear. *Everyone* deserves respect and kindness. You will *never* regret being kind.

What we do for ourselves alone dies with us; what we do for others is timeless. No one is more deceived or cheated than a selfish person.

No man was ever honored for what he received.
Honor has been the reward for what he gave.
—CALVIN COOLIDGE

Invest in the success of others. When you help someone up a mountain, you'll find yourself close to the summit as well.

Proverbs says, "It is possible to give away and become richer! It is also possible to hold on too tightly and lose everything. Yes, the liberal man shall be rich! By watering others, he waters himself" (11:24–25 TLB).

What I gave, I have;
What I spent, I had;
What I kept, I lost.
—OLD EPITAPH

You and I were created to help others. If you treat a person as they are, they will remain the same. If you treat them as if they were what they could be, they can become what they could be. Practicing the Golden Rule is not a sacrifice; it's an incredible investment.

You grow to the extent that you give out. By giving out, you create more room to grow on the inside. So don't give till it hurts; give till it feels good. Make this commitment:

I will leave others better than I found them.

If you want others to improve, let them hear the nice things you say about them. People will treat you the way you view them. Find the good in everyone; draw out their talents and abilities. To lead people, let them know that you are behind them. It is the duty of all leaders to make it difficult for others to do wrong, easy to do right.

What means most in life is what you have done for others. Most people can smile for two months on five words of praise and a pat on the back. The best way to encourage yourself is to encourage someone else.

> *Those who bring sunshine to the lives of others cannot keep it from themselves.*
>
> —James Matthew Barrie

CHANGE IS HERE TO STAY

THE LATE ASTRONAUT JAMES IRWIN said, "You might think going to the moon was the most scientific project ever, but they literally 'threw us' in the direction of the moon. We had to adjust our course every ten minutes and landed only fifty feet inside of the 500-mile radius of our target." On that mission, every change, no matter how small, was essential to success.

Max DePree advised, "When you can't change the direction of the wind—adjust your sails." We cannot become what we need to be by remaining what we are. People hate change, yet it's the only thing that brings growth. There is nothing so permanent as change.

Everyone wants to change the world, but no one thinks of changing himself.

> *He who ignores discipline comes to poverty and shame, but whoever heeds correction is honored.*
> —PROVERBS 13:18

The road to success is always under construction. Non-acceptance of your present creates a future. "Better to be pruned to grow than cut up to burn," said John Trapp. A bad habit never goes away by itself.

> *[Change is] always an undo-it-yourself project.*
> —ABIGAIL VAN BUREN

Wise people sometimes change their minds—fools never do. Be open to changes in your plans. It is a sign of strength to make changes when necessary.

The longer a person is in error, the surer he is that he's right, and the less open he is to change. Defending your faults and errors only proves that you have no intention of quitting them. *An obstinate man does not hold opinions—they hold him.*

Where we cannot invent we can at least improve. A "sensational new idea" is sometimes just an old idea with its sleeves rolled up. If you itch for ideas, keep on scratching. Don't be afraid of change.

Almost all people are in favor of *progress;* it's the *change* they don't like. Face it, constant change is here to stay. Most people become willing to change not because they see the light but because they feel the heat.

Great ideas still need change, adaptation, and modification in order to prosper and succeed. Henry Ford forgot to put a reverse gear in his first automobile (it would get you there, but there was no backing up if you went too far). Few knew of his oversight, but because he changed it, there are few who *don't* know of his success. Success and growth are unlikely if you always do things the way you've always done them. When you stop changing, you stop growing.

YOUR WORDS REFLECT WHAT YOU
BELIEVE ABOUT YOUR FUTURE

CONSIDER THE CASE OF the Illinois man who left the snow-filled streets of Chicago for a vacation in Florida. His wife was on a business trip and was planning to meet him there the next day. When he reached his hotel, he decided to send her a quick e-mail. Unable to find the scrap of paper on which he'd written her e-mail address, he did his best to type it in from memory.

Unfortunately, he missed one letter, and his note was directed instead to an elderly preacher's wife, whose husband had passed away only the day before. When the grieving widow checked her e-mail, she took one look at the monitor, let out a piercing scream, and fell to the floor in a dead faint. At the sound, her family rushed into the room and saw this note on the screen:

> *Dearest Wife,*
> *Just got checked in. Everything's prepared for your arrival tomorrow.*
> *P.S. Sure is hot down here.*

What we say and who we say it to make a big difference. Ignorance is always eager to speak. The best time to hold your tongue is when you feel you must say something. You're unlikely to be hurt by anything you didn't say. Never judge a person's horsepower by their exhaust. *Some people speak from experience; others, from experience, don't speak.*

We all should take a tip from nature—our ears aren't made to shut, but our mouth is! When an argument flares up, the wise person quenches it with silence. Silence is the ultimate weapon of power; it is also one of the hardest arguments to dispute. Sometimes you have to be quiet to be heard.

The person who finds the negative seldom finds anything else. Live your life as an exclamation, not an explanation. Children are born optimists, then the world slowly tries to educate them out of their "delusion." The fact is, the more you complain the less you'll obtain. A life of complaining is the ultimate rut. The only difference between a rut and a grave is the timing.

Some people always find the bad in a situation. Do you know people like that? How many successful complainers do you know? "Little men with little minds and little imagination go through life in little ruts, smugly resisting all changes that would jar their little worlds" (Anonymous). Small things affect small minds.

Just to see how it feels, for the next twenty-four hours refrain from saying anything bad about anyone or anything. Mark Twain said,

> *The difference between the right word and almost the right word is the difference between lightning and the lightning bug.*

Has your dream become your hope, or your excuse? Don't complain. The wheel that squeaks the loudest often gets replaced. Flapping gums dull two of your important senses—

audio and visual. Many a great idea has been quenched by wrong words. Don't spend your life standing at the complaint counter.

A wise old owl sat on an oak;
The more he saw the less he spoke;
The less he spoke the more he heard;
Why aren't we like that wise old bird?

—EDWARD H. RICHARDS

THE PERSON WHO EXPECTS NOTHING WILL NEVER BE DISAPPOINTED

B E BOLD AND COURAGEOUS. When you look back on your life, you'll regret the things you didn't do more than the ones you did. When facing a difficult task, act as though it is impossible to fail. If you're going to climb Mount Everest, bring along the American flag. Go out on a limb—that's where the fruit is.

Go from looking at what you can see to believing what you can have. Here's some life-changing advice: Don't undertake a plan unless it is distinctly important and nearly impossible. Don't bunt—aim out of the ballpark.

The mediocre man thinks he isn't, but Ronald E. Osborn recommends, "Undertake something that is difficult; it will do you good. Unless you try to do something beyond what you have already mastered, you will never grow."

Not doing more than the average is what keeps the average down.

—WILLIAM M. WINANS

It is difficult to say what is truly impossible, for what we take for granted today seemed impossible yesterday. "*Impossible*," Napoleon is quoted as saying, "is a word found only in the dictionary of fools." What words are found in your dictionary?

He who is afraid of doing too much always does too little. To achieve all that is possible, we must attempt the impossible. Your vision must be bigger than you. Learn to be comfortable with great dreams.

The best jobs haven't been found. The best work hasn't been done. Unless you take on more than you can possibly do, you will never do all that you can. Don't listen to those who say, "It's not done that way." Don't listen to those who say, "You're taking too big a chance." Develop an infinite capacity to ignore what others say can't be done. In the first chapter of Joshua, the Lord says three times to him, "Be strong and courageous." I believe He is still saying this to us today.

If Michelangelo had painted the floor instead of the ceiling of the Sistine Chapel, it would surely be rubbed out by now. "Always aim high, going after things that will make a difference, rather than seeking the safe path of mediocrity," says Wes Roberts.

Don't bother with small plans, because they motivate no one (especially you)! The person who expects nothing will never be disappointed. After Roger Bannister ran the first sub-four-minute mile, thirty-seven others followed suit within one year; within two years, *three hundred* had also achieved it. Thinking high affects others.

The most disappointed people in the world are those who get just what is coming to them and no more. There are a lot of ways to become a failure, but never taking a chance is the most successful.

When You Stretch the Truth, It Always Snaps Back to Hurt You

A FOUR-YEAR-OLD WAS AT the pediatrician for a checkup. As the doctor looked down her ears with an otoscope, he asked, "Do you think I'll find Big Bird in here?" The little girl stayed silent. Next, the doctor took a tongue depressor and looked down her throat. He asked, "Do you think I'll find the Cookie Monster down there?" Again, the little girl was silent. Then the doctor put a stethoscope to her chest. As he listened to her heartbeat, he asked, "Do you think I'll hear Barney in there?" "Oh, no!" the little girl replied. "Jesus is in my heart. Barney's on my underpants."

Tell it like it is. Do the right thing. Commit yourself to excellence from the start. No legacy is so rich as excellence. The quality of your life will be in direct proportion to your commitment to excellence, regardless of what you choose to do.

It's a funny thing about life: if you refuse to accept anything but the best, you very often get it.
—W. Somerset Maugham

It takes less time to do something right than it does to

explain why you did it wrong. There is no right way to do the wrong thing. "There is an infinite difference between a little wrong and just right, between fairly good and the best, between mediocrity and superiority," said Orison Marden.

Every day we should ask ourselves, "Why should I be hired instead of someone else?" or "Why should people do business with me instead of my competitors?" Frank Outlaw says,

Watch your actions; they become habits. Watch your habits; they become character. Watch your character; it becomes your destiny.

To be excellent, be honest. Those who are given to white lies soon become color-blind. When you stretch the truth, watch out for the snap back. Again: A lie has no legs to support itself—it requires other lies. Beware of a half-truth; you may get ahold of the wrong half.

Each time you are honest, you propel yourself toward greater success. Each time you lie, even a little white lie, you push yourself toward failure.

Outside forces don't control your character; you do. *The measure of a person's real character is what he would do if he knew he would never be found out.*

In the race for excellence, there is no finish line. Be more concerned with your character than with your reputation. Your character is what you really are, while your reputation is merely what others think you are.

"He that is good will infallibly become better, and he that is bad will as certainly become worse; for vice, virtue, and time are three things that never stand still," said Charles Caleb Colton. Recently I saw a plaque that said,

Excellence can be attained if you . . .
Care more than others think is wise,
Risk more than others think is safe,
Dream more than others think is practical,
Expect more than others think is possible.

Excellence—it's contagious. Start an epidemic!

Don't Let Regrets Replace Your Dreams

I N THE LATTER PART of the nineteenth century, when the Methodist Church was holding its denominational convention, one leader stood up and shared his vision both for the church and society at large. He told the ministers and evangelists how he believed someday men would fly from place to place instead of merely traveling on horseback. It was a concept too outlandish for many members of his audience to handle.

One minister, Bishop Wright, stood up and angrily protested. "Heresy!" he shouted. "Flight is reserved for the angels!" He went on to elaborate that if God had intended for man to fly, He would have given him wings. Clearly, the bishop was unable to envision what the speaker was predicting.

When Bishop Wright finished his brief protest, he gathered up his two sons, Orville and Wilbur, and left the auditorium. That's right. His sons were Orville and Wilbur Wright. Several years later, on December 17, 1903, those two sons did what their father called impossible: they recorded the first human flight (four times).

Yesterday ended last night. So today it is more valuable to look ahead and prepare than to look back and regret.

A man is not old until regrets take the place of dreams.

—John Barrymore

Regret looks back. Worry looks around. Vision looks up.

Life can be understood backward, but it must be lived forward. If past history were all that mattered, librarians would be the only successful people in the world. The past should only be viewed with gratitude for the good things. So look backward with gratitude and look forward with confidence. Your past is the start of your fresh start.

Consider what Vivian Laramore Rader said: "I've shut the door on yesterday and thrown the key away—tomorrow holds no fears for me, since I've found today." Use the past as a launching pad, not a lawn chair. Dreams of the future are more valuable than the history of the past.

Experience is at best yesterday's answer to today's problem. Your past is not your potential. Never build your future around your past. The past is over. To succeed, you must be willing to shed part of your previous life.

Daniel Meacham cautions, "Keep your eye on the road, and use your rear-view mirror only to avoid trouble." Stop taking journeys into the past. Don't make the mistake of letting yesterday use up too much of today.

It is more valuable to look where you're going than to see where you've been. Don't view your future only from the perspective of yesterday. It's too easy to limit everything and hinder the dream within you. "The past should be a springboard, not a hammock," said Edmund Burke. You can never plan the future by looking at the past. Those to whom yesterday still looks big aren't doing much today.

Your future contains more happiness than any past you can remember. Don't look at your past to determine your future.

You can't walk backward into the future. True misery can be found by being a yesterday person trying to get along in a tomorrow world. Don't let your past mistakes become memorials. They should be cremated, not embalmed.

Those who predominantly talk about the past are going backward. Those who talk about the present are usually just maintaining. But those who talk about the future are growing. The more you look backward, the less you'll see what's ahead for you.

Some people stay so far in the past that the future is gone before they get there. The future frightens only those who prefer living in the past. No one has ever backed into prosperity. You can't have a better tomorrow if you are thinking about yesterday today. Yesterday has passed forever and is beyond our control. What lies behind us is insignificant compared to what lies ahead.

BECOME AN AUTHORITY
ON SOMETHING

O PPORTUNITY IS ALL AROUND YOU. What matters is where you put your focus. Ask yourself this question every day: "Where should my focus be?" Where you focus your attention, you create strength and momentum.

These are the characteristics of momentum:

(1) It is single-minded;
(2) it is unwavering in the pursuit of a goal;
(3) it has passion that knows no limits;
(4) it demands a concentrated intensity and a definite sense of destiny; and most of all,
(5) it has a boundless vision and commitment to excellence.

Concentration is the key that opens the door to accomplishment:

The first law of success . . . is concentration—to bend all the energies to one point, and to go directly to that point, looking neither to the right nor to the left.
—WILLIAM MATTHEWS

The most successful people have always been those of concentration, who have struck their blows in one place until they have accomplished their purpose. They are of one specific idea, one steady aim, and one single and concentrated purpose.

There is a great distance between most people's dreams and the results they achieve; this is due to the difference in their commitment to bring together all the options of their ability and to focus them upon one point.

There are two quick ways to disaster: taking nobody's advice and taking everybody's advice. Learn to say no to the good so you can say yes to the best. A. P. Goethe said that in order to succeed, you must know three things: "(1) what to eliminate; (2) what to preserve; and (3) when to say no, for developing the power to say no gives us the capacity to say yes."

We accomplish things by directing our desires, not by ignoring them. What an immense power you will have over your life when you possess distinct aims. Your words, the tone of your voice, your dress, and your very motions change and improve when you begin to live for a reason.

Don't be a person who is uncertain about the future and hazy about the present. Stay in the groove without making it a rut. Make something your specialty; you cannot find until you define. To finish the race, stay on the track.

I am astonished at the aimlessness of most people's lives. As a result of a lack of focus, they delegate the direction of their lives to others. Don't live your life like that. Instead,

Learn to define yourself, to content yourself with some specific thing and some definite work; dare to be what you really are, and to learn to accept with good grace all that you are not.

—Anonymous

Spend Your Time and Energy Creating, Not Criticizing

A KINDERGARTEN TEACHER was observing her classroom of children while they drew, occasionally walking around to see each child's artwork. As she got to one little girl who was laboring diligently, she asked what the drawing was.

The girl replied, "I'm drawing God."

The teacher paused and said, "But no one knows what God looks like."

Without missing a beat or looking up from her drawing, the girl replied, "They will in a minute."

People with momentum all share one trait: they attract criticism. How you respond to that criticism will determine the rate of your momentum. I was reading a cover story on Billy Graham in *Time* magazine recently and was surprised to find several criticisms of him from fellow ministers. I was reminded of this fact: All great people get great criticism. Learn to accept and expect the unjust criticisms for your great goals and accomplishments.

It can be beneficial to receive constructive criticism from those who have your best interests at heart, but you're not responsible to respond to those who don't. Don't ever give time to a critic; instead, invest it with a friend. I like what Edward Gibbon said:

> *I never make the mistake of arguing with people for whose opinions I have no respect.*

It's a thousand times easier to criticize than to create. That's why critics are never problem solvers:

> *Any fool can criticize, condemn and complain, and most do.*
>
> —DALE CARNEGIE

My feeling is that the person who says it cannot be done shouldn't interrupt the one who's doing it. Just remember, when you're kicked from behind, it means you're out in front. A Yiddish proverb says, "A critic is like the girl who can't dance so she says the band can't play."

Critics know the answers without having probed deep enough to really know the questions:

> *A critic is a man created to praise greater men than himself, but he is never able to find them.*
>
> —RICHARD LE GALLIENNE

The critic is convinced that the chief purpose of sunshine is to cast shadows. He doesn't usually believe anything, but he still wants you to believe him. Like a cynic, he always knows the "price of everything and the value of nothing" (Oscar Wilde). Don't waste time responding to your critics, because you owe nothing to them.

Don't belittle—be big, and don't become a critic.

We have no more right to put our discordant states of mind into the lives of those around us and rob them of their sunshine and brightness than we have to enter their houses and steal their silverware.

—JULIA SETON

In criticizing others, remember that you will work overtime for no pay.

Never throw mud. If you do, you may hit your mark, but you will have dirty hands. Don't be a cloud because you failed to become a star. Instead, "Give so much time to the improvement of yourself that you have no time to criticize others" (from the Optimist Creed). *Spend your time and energy creating, not criticizing.*

A good thing to remember,
A better thing to do—
Work with the construction gang,
Not the wrecking crew.

—ANONYMOUS

MOMENTUM DOESN'T JUST HAPPEN

People judge you by your actions, not your intentions. You may have a heart of gold, but so does a hard-boiled egg.

—GOOD READING

A thousand words will not leave as lasting an impression as one deed. Connect your good intentions with awesome actions. If you don't do it, you don't really believe it.

Some people spend their whole time searching for what's right, but then they can't seem to find any time to practice it. Remember, knowing what is right to do and then not doing it is wrong. Your life story is not written with a pen but with your actions. To *do* nothing is the way to *be* nothing.

Action subdues fear. "When we challenge our fears, we master them. When we wrestle with our problems, they lose their grip on us. When we dare to confront the things that scare us, we open the door to personal liberty" (Anonymous).

> *The common conception is that motivation leads to action, but the reverse is true—action precedes motivation.*
>
> —ROBERT J. MCKAIN

Don't wait to be motivated: Michael Cadena says, "Take the bull by the horns until you have him screaming for mercy."

Laziness is a load. Expectation is the idle man's income. Ironically, idleness is persistent. It keeps on and on, but soon enough it arrives at poverty. Nothing is more exhausting than searching for easy ways to earn a living.

"There is no idleness without a thousand troubles" (Welsh creed). We are weakest when we try to get something for nothing. Proverbs says, "Hard work means prosperity; only fools idle away their time" (12:11 NLT).

"Shun idleness. It is a rust that attaches itself to the most brilliant of metals" (François Voltaire). Henry Ford once commented,

> *You can't build a reputation on what you're going to do.*

We need to be like a cross between a carrier pigeon and a woodpecker: not only carrying the message but also knocking on the door.

I believe we live in an unfinished world so we might share in the joys and satisfaction of creation. Creativity is built into every one of us; it's part of our design. Each of us lives less of the life intended for us when we choose not to use the creative powers we possess.

"I'm a big fan of dreams. Unfortunately, dreams are the first casualty in life—people seem to give them up quicker than anything for a 'reality'" (Kevin Costner). Hans Selye noted,

Realistic people with practical aims are rarely as real-istic or practical in the long-run of life as the dream-ers who pursue their dreams.

What you need is an idea. Be brave enough to live creatively.

A man of words and not of deeds is like a flower bed full of weeds. Don't let weeds grow around your dreams. To only dream of the person you would like to be is to waste the person you are. Don't just dream of great accomplishments; stay awake and do them.

BEGIN SOMEWHERE

PASTOR JOHNSON ANSWERS HIS PHONE.
"Hello, is this Pastor Johnson?"
"It is."
"This is the IRS. Can you help us?"
"I can."
"Do you know a Bill Wilcox?"
"I do."
"Is he a member of your congregation?"
"He is."
"Did he donate $10,000?"
"He will."

What you can do—you can do. What works? Work on that. Don't wish you could do things you can't do. Instead, think of what you can do.

Everyone who got where he is, had to begin where he was. Only one person in a thousand knows how to really live in the present. The problem is that we seldom think of what we have; instead, we think of what we lack.

"We don't need more strength or more ability or greater opportunity. What we need to use is what we have" (Basil Walsh). People are always ignoring something they can do and trying to do something they can't. Learning new things won't help the person who isn't using what he already knows. Success means doing the best we can with what we have.

Norman Vincent Peale said,

> *We've all heard that we have to learn from our mistakes, but I think it is more important to learn from our successes. If you learn only from your mistakes, you are inclined to learn only errors.*

In fact, some people spend their whole lives failing and never even notice.

The main thing that's wrong with doing nothing is that you never know when you are finished. When you are through improving, you're through. Use whatever you have been given, and more will come to you. Never leave well enough alone.

"You can't control the weather, but you can control the moral atmosphere that surrounds you. Why worry about things you can't control? Get busy controlling the things that depend upon you" (*In a Nutshell*). Orison Marden says, "A strong, successful man is not the victim of his environment. He creates favorable conditions." The person who gets ahead is the one who does more than is necessary—and keeps on doing it.

DARE TO REACH BEYOND YOURSELF

PEOPLE NEARLY ALWAYS PICK a problem their own size and ignore or leave to others the bigger or smaller ones. Pick a problem that's bigger than you. "Success, real success, in any endeavor demands more from an individual than most people are willing to offer—not more than they are capable of offering" (James Roche).

The desire for safety stands against every great and virtuous dream. Security, many times, is the first step toward stagnation. Boldness in vision is the first, second, and third most important thing. If you dare nothing you should expect nothing.

Christian Bovee noted, "One who is contented with what he has done will never be famous for what he will do." If you have achieved all you have planned for yourself, you haven't planned enough.

Be used for something significant. Dare to do what's right for you. Choose a goal for which you are willing to exchange a piece of your life.

The surest way to happiness is to lose yourself in a cause greater than yourself. You'll be unhappy if you do not reach for something beyond yourself. If God is your partner, make your plans *big*.

It is difficult to say what is impossible, for the dream of yesterday is the hope of today and the reality of to-morrow.

—ROBERT GODDARD

Every great action is impossible when it's undertaken. Only after it's accomplished does it seem possible to the average man.

To small thinkers, everything looks like a mountain. The grandest things are, in some ways, the easiest to do because there is so little competition.

To be completely satisfied with yourself is a sure sign that progress is about to end. If you are satisfied with yourself, you'd better change your ideals. Gilbert Caplin said, "How much better to know that we have dared to live our dreams than to live our lives in a lethargy of regret."

You'll never succeed beyond your wildest dreams unless you have some wild dreams.

"Comfort Zone"

I used to have a Comfort Zone
Where I knew I couldn't fail;
The same four walls of busy work
Were really more like jail.

I longed so much to do the things
I'd never done before,
But I stayed inside my Comfort Zone
And paced the same old floor.

I said it didn't matter,
That I wasn't doing much;
I said I didn't care for things
Like dreams, goals and such.

I claimed to be so busy
With the things inside my zone,
But deep inside I longed for
Something special of my own.

I couldn't let my life go by,
Just watching others win.
I held my breath and stepped outside
And let the change begin.

I took a step and with new strength
I'd never felt before,
I kissed my Comfort Zone "good-bye"
And closed and locked the door.

If you are in a Comfort Zone,
Afraid to venture out,
Remember that all winners were
At one time filled with doubt.

A step of faith and the Word of God,
Can make your dreams come true.
Greet your future with a smile,
Success is there for you!

—AUTHOR UNKNOWN; SOURCE UNKNOWN

STRONG CONVICTIONS PRECEDE GREAT ACTIONS

I N *THE SOWER'S SEEDS,* Brian Cavanaugh tells the story of how Edmund Hillary was the first man to climb Mount Everest. On May 29, 1953, he scaled the highest mountain then known to man: more than 29,000 feet above sea level. He was knighted for his efforts. He even made American Express card commercials because of it! However, until we read his book, *High Adventure,* we don't understand that Hillary had to grow into this success. You see, in 1952, he attempted to climb Mount Everest but failed. A few weeks later a group in England asked him to address its members.

Edmund Hillary walked onstage to a thunderous applause. The audience was recognizing an attempt at greatness, but Hillary saw himself as a failure. He moved away from the microphone and walked to the edge of the platform. He made a fist and pointed at a picture of the mountain. He said in a loud voice,

> *Mount Everest, you beat me the first time, but I'll beat you the next time because you've grown all you are going to grow . . . and I'm still growing!*

The world makes room for a person of purpose. His words and actions demonstrate that he knows where he's going. You are built to conquer circumstances, solve problems, and attain goals. You'll find no real satisfaction or happiness in life without obstacles to conquer, goals to achieve, and a purpose to fulfill.

You were made on purpose, for a purpose. People say they want riches; what they need is fulfillment of a purpose. Happiness comes when we abandon ourselves for a purpose.

In your heart there is a sleeping lion called *purpose*. Every person alive has a destiny. Be on a mission. Have a definite sense of direction and purpose for your life. Successful lives are motivated by dynamic purpose.

As soon as you resign yourself to fate, your resignation is promptly accepted. You don't have a fate; you have a purpose. When you look into the future, you'll see it's so bright it'll make you squint. I'm encouraged by George Eliot, who said,

It's never too late to be what you might have been.

Billy Sunday observed, "More men fail through lack of purpose than lack of talent." If your method is "hit or miss," you'll usually miss, because "if you're not sure where you are going, you'll probably end up someplace else" (Robert Mager).

Don't be a person who doesn't know where you're going; be on your way. Growth for the sake of growth is the ideology of the cancer cell. *Go forward with definite purpose.*

Lord Chesterfield wrote,

Firmness of purpose is one of the most necessary sinews of character and one of the best instruments of success. Without it, genius wastes its efforts in a maze of inconsistencies.

The person who has no direction is a slave of his circumstances. The poorest person is not without money but without purpose. Without purpose, the only thing you can do is grow older.

David Burns advised, "If you don't have a vision for your life, then you probably haven't focused in on anything." In the absence of vision there can be no clear and constant focus.

Once your purpose is clear, decisions will jump at you. "When you discover your mission, you will feel its demand. It will fill you with enthusiasm and a burning desire to get to work on it" (W. Clement Stone).

THE REWARD FOR CONFORMITY WAS THAT EVERYONE LIKED YOU EXCEPT YOURSELF

—Rita Mae Brown

DO YOU WANT TO STAND out in the world? Then be yourself. Be what you really are. This is the first step toward becoming better than what you are now.

You and I are born equal but also different:

> *No man could be ideally successful until he has found his place. Like a locomotive, he is strong on the track, but weak anywhere else.*
>
> —ORISON MARDEN

Choose to become yourself.

Avoid following the crowd. Be an engine, not a caboose. Herman Melville wrote, "It is better to fail in originality than to succeed in imitation." *Average people would rather be wrong than be different.*

Conformity is the enemy of growth and satisfaction. Did

you know you're destined to be different? Dare to be different and follow your own star.

Ask yourself these questions: If I try to be like him, who will be like me? If I'm not me, who will I be? The more you develop your potential, the less you will become like someone else. As long as you are trying to be like someone else, the best you can ever be is number two.

Trying to be like someone else is self-defeating. One of your main purposes in life is to give birth to yourself. Depend on the wisdom of the book of Romans: God has given each of us an ability to do certain things well.

We can't reach our destiny taking another man's road. If you never walk except where you see another person's tracks, you will make no new discoveries for yourself.

> *Do not follow where the path may lead—go instead where there is no path and leave a trail.*
> —UNKNOWN

Don't be common. The common go nowhere. You must be uncommon to be a champion. Have you ever noticed that almost every very successful person is a little "different"? Your responsibility is not to remake yourself but to make the absolute best of what you're made of.

Don't compromise yourself . . . you're all you've got:

> *Almost every man wastes part of his life in attempts to display qualities he does not possess.*
> —SAMUEL JOHNSON

Don't let your life be a continual struggle to be what you are not and to do what you should not.

"The more you are like yourself, the less you are like anyone else" (Walt Disney). And the more you're like Jesus, the more you'll become like you're supposed to be. You're like a tree— you must put forth the fruit that's created in you.

"I Used to Be Indecisive, but Now I'm Not Sure"

D O YOU SAY THIS?
Decisions are what transform an idea into a reality. Your destiny is not a matter of chance; it is a matter of choice. Many people have the right aims in life—they just never get around to pulling the trigger. You have to know what you want in order to attain it.

Harvey Cox said, "Not to decide is to decide." Weeds grow easily in the soil of indecision. Get out of the middle of the road. Standing in the middle of the road is very dangerous; you can get knocked down by traffic going both directions. The train of failure runs on the track of indecision.

Because of indecision, you can die before you're actually dead.

Indecision is debilitating; it feeds upon itself; it is, one might say, habit forming. Not only that, but it is contagious; it transmits itself to others.

—H. A. HOPF

A man with one watch knows what time it is; a man with

two is never quite sure. Until you are decisively committed, there is hesitancy and the chance to draw back, followed by ineffectiveness. Listen to what you say. If you hear yourself saying, "I've decided," you're on the path toward an exciting and productive life.

Leaders have wills, not just wishes. The greater the degree of wishful thinking, the greater the degree of mediocrity. The weak are always forced to decide between alternatives that others have set before them instead of the ones they've chosen for themselves. This lifestyle will leave you unhappy; however, consider what Mike Murdock says:

> *You have no right to complain about what you permit.*

A wise person makes his own decisions; an ignorant one follows public opinion. Don't worry about not making a decision; someone else will make it for you. You are where you are today because of the choices you've made and haven't made.

> *The average man does not know what to do with this life, yet wants another one that will last forever.*
> —ANATOLE FRANCE

Results and success follow commitment and decisions. The result is that one decisive person always accomplishes more than a hundred people with just an interest.

Be decisive even if it means you'll sometimes be wrong. A key to your future is that you can still choose, you can still decide. What you commit yourself to be will change you from what you are into what you can be. Decision determines destiny.

WHEN YOU FALL, PICK SOMETHING UP

ANYBODY WHO IS CURRENTLY ACHIEVING anything in life is simultaneously risking failure. Failure is often the first necessary step toward success. If we don't risk failing, we won't get the chance to succeed. When we are trying, we are winning. Babe Ruth said, "Never let the fear of striking out get in your way" (only one player, Hank Aaron, has hit more homers than Ruth, but seventy players have had more strikeouts).

The greatest mistake you can make in life is to continually fear you will make one.

> *Don't be afraid to fail. Don't waste energy trying to cover up failure. If you're not failing, you're not growing.*
>
> —H. STANLEY JUDD

Successful people stop growing and learning when they become less and less willing to risk failure. Failure is delay, not defeat. We all make mistakes—*especially* those who act. Again, the only ones who are never disappointed are those who don't expect anything.

Stop trying to be perfect. When you have a serious decision to make, tell yourself firmly you are going to make it. Don't expect that it will be a perfect one. I love the wisdom of Winston Churchill:

The maxim "Nothing avails but perfection" may be spelled p-a-r-a-l-y-s-i-s.

Henry Ward Beecher wrote, "I don't like these cold, precise, perfect people who in order not to speak wrong, never speak at all, and in order not to do wrong, never do anything." The pursuit of excellence is gratifying and healthy; the pursuit of perfection is frustrating, unproductive, and wasteful.

The fact is that you're like a tea bag: You won't know your own strength until you've been through some hot water. Mistakes are something we can avoid only by saying nothing, doing nothing, and being nothing.

Remember, there are two benefits of failure. First, if you do fail, you learn what doesn't work; and second, the failure gives you an opportunity to try a new approach.... Most people think of success and failure as opposites, but they are actually both products of the same process.

—ROGER VON OECH

Some defeats are only installments to victory. Henry Ford noted, "Even a mistake may turn out to be the one thing necessary to a worthwhile achievement." Some people learn from their mistakes; some never recover from them. Learn how to fail intelligently. Develop success from failure.

It is better to fail in doing something than to excel in doing nothing. Mistakes and failure are two of the surest stepping-stones to success. Your season of failure is the best time for sowing your seeds of success.

> *No matter what mistakes you have made—no matter how you've messed things up—you can still make a new beginning. The person who fully realizes this suffers less from the shock and pain of failure and sooner gets off to a new beginning.*
> —NORMAN VINCENT PEALE

Successful people are not afraid to fail. They go from failure to failure until at last success is theirs. One of the best ways to accelerate your success is to double your failure rate. The law of failure is one of the most powerful of all success laws.

BE THE FIRST TO FORGIVE

IF YOU WANT TO TRAVEL far and fast, travel light. Unpack all of your envy, bitterness, resentment, rage, and fear. Never reject forgiveness or the opportunity to forgive. The weak can never forgive because forgiveness is a characteristic of the strong. Lawrence Sterne said, "Only the brave know how to forgive. . . . A coward never forgives; it is not in his nature."

Living a life of unforgiveness is like leaving the parking brake on when you drive your car: It's a drag! It causes you to slow down and lose your momentum. Unforgiveness toward someone is one of the most expensive luxuries you can possess. A deep-seated grudge in your life eats away at your peace of mind like a deadly cancer, destroying a vital organ of life. In fact, there are few things as pathetic to behold as the person who has harbored a hateful grudge for many years.

When you live a life of unforgiveness, revenge naturally follows. Revenge is deceptive. It looks sweet, but it's truly bitter. It always costs more to avenge a wrong than to bear it. You never can win by trying to even the score.

Forgiveness is your deepest need and highest achievement. Without forgiveness, life is governed by an endless cycle of resentment and retaliation. What a pathetic waste of effort.

"He who has not forgiven an enemy has never yet tasted one of the most sublime enjoyments of life," declared Johann Lavater. Forgiveness is the key to personal peace. Forgiveness releases you and creates freedom.

One of the secrets of a long and fruitful life is to forgive everybody everything every night before you go to bed. Forgiving those who have wronged you is a key to personal peace. Peter Von Winter said, "It is manlike to punish, but Godlike to forgive." When you have a huge chip on your shoulder, it causes you to lose your balance. When you stop nursing a grudge, it dies. Forgiveness is a funny thing. It warms the heart and cools the sting.

It is far better to forgive and forget than to hate and remember. What really matters is what happens in us, not to us. Josh Billings says,

There is no revenge so complete as forgiveness.

Richard Nixon said, "Those who hate you don't win unless you hate them, and then you destroy yourself." *Unforgiveness blocks blessings; forgiveness releases blessings.*

Do you want to release the past and claim the future? Grab hold of what Paul Boese said:

Forgiveness does not change the past, but it does enlarge the future.

You can be wrong in the middle of being right when you don't forgive someone. "Protest long enough that you are right, and you will be wrong" (Yiddish proverb).

Don't burn bridges; you'll be surprised how many times

you have to cross over that same river. Unforgiveness is empty, but forgiveness makes a future possible. You'll start your day on the right foot if you daily ask yourself, "Whom do I need to forgive?"

People Who Take Risks Are the People You'll Lose Against

—John Scully

Y OU AND I ARE LIKE RUBBER BANDS: We're most useful when we're stretched. You can only accomplish in proportion to what you attempt. The reason so little is accomplished is generally because so little is attempted.

> *Shoot for the moon. Even if you miss it, you will land among the stars.*
>
> —Les Brown

"It is not because things are difficult that we do not dare; it is because we do not dare that things are difficult" (Seneca). The definition of impossible: "Something nobody can do until somebody does." Never say never. You have to think big to be big.

The fact is, it's fun to do the impossible. When we're playing it safe, we create the most insecurity. Therefore, look at things *as they can be.*

You do not tap the talents inside you until you attempt the

impossible. Risk is part of every success plan: "Mediocre minds usually dismiss anything that reaches beyond their own understanding" (Francois de la Rochefoucauld).

Calvin Coolidge said, "We do not need more intellectual power, we need more spiritual power. We do not need more things that are seen, we need more of the things that are unseen." Paul told the Philippians,

> *I can do everything God asks me to with the help*
> *of Christ who gives me the strength and power.*
> *(4:13* TLB*)*

Look for ways to exercise your risk muscle. Everyone has a risk muscle, and you keep it in the proper shape by experimenting and trying new things. Bite off more than you can chew.

Robert Schuller states, "The people who are really failures are the people who set their standards so low, keep the bar at such a safe level, that they never run the risk of failure." Unless you enter the beehive, you can't take the honey.

A great ship always asks for deep water. When you dare for nothing, hope for nothing. Progress always involves risk. You can't steal second base and keep your foot on first. He who does not dare will not get his share.

IT IS MORE BLESSED TO GIVE ...
THAN ANYTHING

*Nobody cares how much you know until they know
how much you care.*

—THEODORE ROOSEVELT

Life is a lot like the game of tennis. Those who don't serve
well end up losing.

A man asked Dr. Karl Menninger, "What would you advise
a person to do if he felt a nervous breakdown coming on?"
Most people expected him to reply, "Consult a psychiatrist." To
their astonishment he replied, "Lock up your house, go across
the railroad tracks, find someone in need and do something to
help that person."

Mother Teresa warned, "Unless life is lived for others, it is
not worthwhile. A self-centered life is totally empty." If you are
dissatisfied with your lot in life, build a *service* station on it. A
good way to forget your troubles is to help others out of theirs.

Serving others is never entirely unselfish, because the giver
always receives. Proverbs says, "Your own soul is nourished
when you are kind; it is destroyed when you are cruel" (11:17

NLT). Think about what questions you will be asked at the close of your life on earth. Nathan Schaeffer says,

> *The question will not be "How much have you got?" but "How much have you given?" Not "How much have you won?" but "How much have you done?" Not "How much have you saved?" but "How much have you sacrificed?" It will be "How much have you loved and served?" not "How much were you honored?"*

Before looking for a way to get, look for a way to give. W. E. Gladstone observed, "Selfishness is the greatest curse of the human race." Self-interest is a fire that consumes others and then itself.

Almost all of our unhappiness is the result of selfishness. Instead, think in terms of what the other person wants, not just what you want. It is absolutely true that you can succeed best and quickest by helping others succeed.

> *The measure of life is not in its duration, but in its donation. Everyone can be great because everyone can serve.*
>
> —PETER MARSHALL

When you are serving others, life is no longer meaningless.

"One thing I know; the only ones among you who will really be happy are those who have sought and found how to serve" (Albert Schweitzer). You can't help another without helping yourself.

"The Cold Within"

Six humans trapped by happenstance
in black and bitter cold.
Each one possessed a stick of wood,
or so the story's told.

Their dying fire in need of logs,
The first woman held hers back.
For of the faces around the fire,
She noticed one was black.

The next man looking 'cross the way
Saw one not of his church,
And couldn't bring himself to give
The fire his stick of birch.

The third man sat in tattered clothes;
He gave his coat a hitch.
Why should his log be put to use
To warm the idle rich?

The rich man just sat back and thought
Of the wealth he had in store,
And how to keep what he had earned
From the lazy, shiftless poor.

The black man's face bespoke revenge
As the fire passed from his sight,
For all he saw in his stick of wood
Was a chance to spite the white.

And the last man of this forlorn group
Did naught except for gain.
Giving only to those who gave
Was how he played the game.

The logs held tight in death's stilled hands
Was proof of human sin—
They didn't die from the cold without,
They died from the cold within.
                            —ANONYMOUS

COMPARISON DOESN'T
PROVE A THING

Every man must do two things alone: he must do his own believing and his own dying.

—MARTIN LUTHER

When you compare yourself with others, you will become bitter, vain, or both—there will always be people better or worse than you.

Making comparisons is a sure path to frustration. Joan Welch said, "You can't clear your own fields while counting the rocks on your neighbor's farm." Lois Cory mused, "The grass may be greener on the other side of the fence, but there's probably more of it to mow." Hills look small and green from a long way off.

Once again: It's a waste of time and energy when you compare your life to that of other people. Life is more fun when you don't keep score with others. Success really is simply a matter of doing what you do best and not worrying about what the other person is going to do.

You carry success or failure within yourself. It does not depend on outside conditions. Success in someone else's life does not hurt the chances for success in yours.

Ask yourself this question that Earl Nightingale posed: "Are you motivated by what you really want out of life, or are you mass-motivated?" Make sure you decide what you really want, not what someone else wants for you. Do you say, "I'm good, but not as good as I ought to be," or do you compare and say, "I'm not as bad as a lot of other people"?

The longer you dwell on another's weakness, the more you affect your own mind with unhappiness. You must create your own system and your own plan, or someone else's will limit you. What happens in another person's life, good or bad, has nothing to do with how you are doing in your own life. If I compare myself to John Grisham, I'll never write another book; if I compare myself to Adolf Hitler, I'll think I'm a saint.

Don't necessarily think you're on the right road because it's a well-beaten path. The greatest risk in life is to wait for and depend on others for your security and satisfaction. Don't measure yourself with another man's coat. Don't evaluate yourself through someone else's eyes.

INVEST IN OTHERS

THERE IS A STORY TOLD by Elizabeth Ballard of an elementary teacher many years ago. Her name was Mrs. Thompson. As she stood in front of her fifth grade class on the very first day of school, she told the children a lie. She looked at her students and said that she loved them all the same. But that was impossible, because there in the front row, slumped in his seat, was a little boy named Teddy Stoddard.

Mrs. Thompson had watched Teddy the year before and noticed that he didn't play well with the other children, that his clothes were unkempt, and that he needed a bath. And Teddy could be unpleasant. It got to the point where Mrs. Thompson would actually take delight in marking his papers with a broad red pen, making bold *X*s and then putting a big *F* at the top of his papers.

At the school where Mrs. Thompson taught, she was required to review each child's past records, and she put Teddy's off until last. However, when she reviewed his file, she received a surprise.

Teddy's first grade teacher wrote, "Teddy is a bright child with a ready laugh. He does his work neatly and has good manners. . . . He is a joy to be around."

His second grade teacher wrote, "Teddy is an excellent student, well-liked by his classmates, but he is troubled because his mother has a terminal illness, and life at home must be a struggle."

His third grade teacher wrote, "His mother's death has been hard on him. He tries to do his best, but his father doesn't show much interest, and his home life will soon affect him if some steps aren't taken."

Teddy's fourth grade teacher wrote, "Teddy is withdrawn and doesn't show much interest in school. He doesn't have many friends and sometimes sleeps in class."

By now Mrs. Thompson realized the problem, and she was ashamed of herself. She felt even worse when her students brought her Christmas presents wrapped in bright paper and beautiful ribbons, except for Teddy's. His present was clumsily wrapped in the heavy brown paper of a grocery bag. Mrs. Thompson took pains to open it in the middle of the other presents. A few of the children started to laugh when she found a rhinestone bracelet with some of the stones missing and a bottle of perfume that was only one-quarter full. But she stifled their laughter when she exclaimed how pretty the bracelet was, putting it on, and dabbing some of the perfume on her wrist.

Teddy Stoddard stayed after school that day just long enough to say, "Mrs. Thompson, today you smelled just like my Mom used to." After the children left, she cried for at least an hour. On that very day she quit teaching reading, writing, and arithmetic. Instead, she began to teach children.

Mrs. Thompson paid particular attention to Teddy. As she worked with him, his mind seemed to come alive. The more she encouraged him, the faster he responded. By the end of the year, Teddy had become one of the brightest children in the class and, despite her lie that she would love all the children the same, Teddy became one of her "teacher's pets."

A year later she found a note under her door from Teddy, telling her that she was still the best teacher he ever had in his whole life. Six years went by before she got another note from Teddy. He then wrote that he had finished high school second in his class, and she was still the best teacher he ever had in his whole life.

Four years after that she got another letter, saying that while things had been tough at times, he'd stayed in school, had stuck with it, and would soon graduate from college with highest honors. He assured Mrs. Thompson that she was still the best and favorite teacher he ever had in his whole life.

Then four more years passed and yet another letter came. This time he explained that after he got his bachelor's degree, he decided to go a little further. The letter explained that she was still the best and favorite teacher he ever had. But now his name was a little longer. The letter was signed Theodore F. Stoddard, M.D.

The story doesn't end there. You see, there was an additional letter that spring. Teddy said he'd met a girl and was going to be married. He explained that his father had died a couple of years ago, and he was wondering if Mrs. Thompson might agree to sit in the place at the wedding that was usually reserved for the mother of the groom. Of course Mrs. Thompson did. And guess what? She wore that bracelet, the one with several rhinestones missing. And she made sure she was wearing the perfume that Teddy remembered his mother wearing on their last Christmas together.

They hugged each other, and Dr. "Teddy" Stoddard whispered in Mrs. Thompson's ear, "Thank you, Mrs. Thompson, for believing in me. Thank you so much for making me feel important and showing me that I could make a difference."

Mrs. Thompson, with tears in her eyes, whispered back: "Teddy, you have it all wrong. You were the one who taught me that *I* could make a difference. I didn't know how to teach until I met you."

One of the most exciting decisions you can make is to be on the lookout for opportunities to invest in others. For me, this has been one of the most powerful principles of momentum I've implemented in my life. About ten years ago, driving with my family to Tulsa from St. Louis, I was listening to a Zig Ziglar tape. Zig said,

> *You'll always have everything you want in life if you'll help enough other people get what they want.*

When I heard this statement, literally, something went off inside of me, and I said out loud, "I'm going to do it." That decision to look for ways to help others, to invest in them, changed my life.

I believe that one of the marks of true greatness is to develop greatness in others:

> *There are three keys to more abundant living: caring about others, daring for others, and sharing with others.*
>
> —WILLIAM WARD

I have found that truly great people have the unique perspective that greatness is not deposited in them to stay but rather to flow through them into others. Norman MacEwan said, "We make a living by what we get, but we make a life by what we give." Assign yourself the purpose of making others happy and successful.

People have a way of becoming what you encourage them to be. Ralph Waldo Emerson observed, "Trust men and they will be true to you; treat them greatly and they will show themselves great." Goethe advised,

Treat people as if they were what they ought to be and help them to become what they are capable of being.

Whatever we praise, we increase. There is no investment you can make that will pay you so well as investing in the improvement of others throughout your life. B. C. Forbes says, "The person who renders loyal service in a humble capacity will be chosen for higher responsibilities, just as the biblical servant who multiplied the one pound given by his master was made ruler over ten cities."

There are two types of people in the world: those who come into a room and say, "Here I am!" and those who come in and say, "Ah, there you are!" How do you know a good person? A good person brings out goodness in others. Find happiness by helping others find it.

A good deed bears interest. You cannot hold a light to another's path without brightening your own. Develop greatness in others. Lift people up, don't put them down.

Allan McGinnis says, "There is no more noble occupation in the world than to assist another human being—to help someone succeed."

The true meaning of life is to plant trees under whose shade you do not expect to sit.
—NELSON HENDERSON

The greatest use of your life is to spend it for something and on someone that will outlast it: "If you cannot win, make the one ahead of you break the record" (Jan McKeithen). Invest in others. It pays great dividends.

TIME FLIES, SO GRAB IT

D ON'T BE A PERSON WHO SAYS, "Ready. Aim ... Aim ... Aim ... Aim ..." Don't strike when the iron is cold. As fast as each opportunity presents itself, seize it! No matter how small the opportunity may be, use it!

Do what you need to do when it ought to be done whether you like it or not. "He who hesitates misses the green light, gets bumped in the rear, and loses his parking space" (Herbert Prochnow).

One of the deceptive beliefs of those who live an unproductive life is that today is not an important day. Every day comes to us bearing gifts. Untie its bow, tear into the wrapping, and open it up. Write on your heart every day: Today is the best day of the year.

By the time the hesitant person has learned to play the game, the players have dispersed and the rules have changed. Scratch opportunity when and where it itches. Life is made up of constant calls to action.

John Maxwell notes, "Successful leaders have the courage to take action while others hesitate." You will never know what you can do until you begin. Remember, the moment you say, "I give up," someone else is seeing the same situation and saying, "My, what a great opportunity."

Ultimately, opportunities aren't lost; someone else picks up those that are missed. One secret of success in life is to be ready for opportunity when it comes. Ability is empty apart from opportunity.

Time flies. It's up to you to be the pilot: "Everything comes to him who hustles while he waits" (Thomas Edison). It has been my observation that productive people get ahead during the time that others waste. Make quick use of the moment.

It is later than you think. Be ready now. Life's alarm clock has no snooze button. It doesn't do any good to "stand up and take notice" if you sit down as soon as opportunity passes by. Look at it, size it up, and make a decision. You postpone your life when you can't make up your mind.

William Ward has this recipe for success:

Study while others are sleeping; work while others are loafing; prepare while others are playing; and dream while others are wishing.

There is no time like the present, and there is no present like time. Those who take advantage of their advantage obtain the advantage. Don't find yourself at the end of your life saying, "What a wonderful life I've had! I only wish I'd realized it sooner."

If You Wait, It Will Probably Be Too Late

ONCE UPON A TIME, the devil decided to destroy the world. He called in all his little devils to make the plans. Anger came first and asked to be allowed to do the job by setting brother against brother. He would make people angry with one another, and they would destroy themselves. Then Lust came and offered to go. He would defile minds, turn people into beasts by causing love to disappear. Next, Greed spoke and offered to destroy humankind with the most destructive of passions: uncontrolled desires. Gluttony and Drunkenness offered to disease bodies and minds and then destroy them. Idleness, Hatred, and Envy each claimed that they could do the job.

The devil was not satisfied with any one of them, but then the last assistant came. He said, "I will talk with people persuasively in terms of all that God wants them to be. I will tell them how fine their plans are to be honest, clean, and brave. I will encourage them in the good purposes of life!" The devil was aghast at such talk. However, the assistant continued: "But I will tell them there is no hurry. They can do all of these things tomorrow. I will advise them to wait until conditions become more favorable before they start!" The devil replied, "You are the one who shall go to earth to destroy humankind!" The assistant's name was Procrastination.

Failure's most successful strategy is procrastination. *Now* is the best time to be alive and productive. If you want to make an easy job seem difficult, just keep putting off doing it.

> *We're all fugitives, and the things we didn't do yester-*
> *day are the bloodhounds.*
>
> —PRISM

Said Joseph Newton, "A duty dodged is like a debt unpaid; it is only deferred and we must come back and settle the account at last."

What holds people back?

> *There are those of us who are always "about" to live.*
> *We're waiting until things change, until there is more*
> *time, until we are less tired, until we get a promotion,*
> *until we settle down—until, until, until. It always*
> *seems that there is some major event that must occur*
> *in our lives before we begin living.*
>
> —GEORGE SHEEHAN

One of these days is really *none* of these days. The "sweet by and by" never comes. People who desire but don't act soon find themselves frozen. They make as much progress as a glacier.

About the only thing that comes to a procrastinator is old age. Do today what you want to postpone until tomorrow:

> *Do not allow idleness to deceive you; for while you*
> *give him today, he steals tomorrow from you.*
>
> —CROWQUILL

When you run in place, everyone will pass you by. Nothing is as fatiguing as the eternal hanging-on of an uncompleted task.

When a person gets into a habit of wasting time, he is sure to waste a great deal that does not belong to him. Ben Franklin said, "One day, today, is worth two tomorrows." What may be done at any time will be done at no time. "Life is like a taxi; the meter keeps a-ticking whether you're getting somewhere or standing still" (Lou Erickson). The successful person does the thing that others never get around to. What the fool does in the end, the wise person does in the beginning.

Sam Slick advised, "Don't stand shivering upon the banks; plunge in at once and have it over with." Tomorrow is the busiest day of the week. If there's a hill to climb, don't think that waiting will make it any smaller.

An unsuccessful person takes a hundred steps because he would not take one step at the right time. If possible, make the decision now, even if the action is in the future. A reviewed decision is usually better than one reached at the last moment.

The fool, with all his other thoughts, has this also: he is always getting ready to live.

—Epicurus

He who fiddles around seldom gets to lead the orchestra. Attack procrastination by eliminating all excuses and reasons for not taking decisive and immediate action.

"Tomorrow will I live," the fool does say; tomorrow itself is too late; the wise lived yesterday.

—Martial

Arthur Brisbane pledged, "While the fool is enjoying the little he has, I will hunt for more. The way to hunt for more is to utilize your odd moments. . . . The man who is always killing time is really killing his own chances in life."

EXCELLENCE IS NEVER A SURPRISE

THE PASSENGERS ON A commercial airliner have been seated and are awaiting the cockpit crew to get them under way.

A murmur is heard in the back of the plane, and a few passengers on the aisle glance back to see the pilot and copilot, both wearing large dark sunglasses, making their way up to the cockpit.

However, the pilot is using a white cane, bumping into passengers right and left as he stumbles down the aisle, and the copilot is using a seeing-eye guide dog. As they pass by the rows of passengers there are nervous giggles heard, as people are thinking that it must be some sort of practical joke.

But a few minutes after the cockpit door has closed behind them the engines start spooling up and the airplane taxis out to the runway.

The passengers look at one another with some uneasiness, whispering among themselves and shifting uneasily or gripping the armrests more tightly. As the airplane starts accelerating rapidly, people begin panicking.

Some passengers are praying, and as the plane gets closer and closer to the end of the runway, passengers become more and more hysterical.

Finally, when the airplane has less than a few seconds of runway left, the shouts of horror fill the cabin as everyone screams at once, but at the very last moment the airplane lifts off and is airborne.

Up in the cockpit, the copilot breathes a sigh of relief and turns to the captain: "You know, one of these days the passengers are going to scream too late, and we're going to get killed."

Sometimes you can allow compromise to go a long way without shouting out against it; how far are you willing to go?

Start every task thinking how to do it better than it has ever been done before. William Danforth exhorts, "Start a crusade in your life to dare to be your very best." Become a yardstick of quality. Do the right thing regardless of what others think.

As we have seen, W. Somerset Maugham said, "It is a funny thing about life; if you refuse to accept anything but the best, you very often get it." Think only of the best, work only for the best, and expect only the best. Excellence is never an accident. Thomas Edison ordered, "There is a way to do it better . . . find it."

There's always an excellent way of doing everything. Henry Ward Beecher counseled, "Hold yourself responsible for a higher standard than anybody else expects of you. Never excuse yourself." Most people aren't used to an environment where excellence is expected.

> *It is those who have this imperative demand for the best in their natures and those who will accept nothing short of it, that hold the banners of progress, that set the standards, the ideals for others.*
> —ORISON MARDEN

People will always determine your character by observing what you stand for or fall for.

Don't seek success. Instead, seek excellence, and you will find both. Work to become, not to acquire. Do the very best you can, and leave the results to take care of themselves. People are funny: they spend money they don't have to buy things they don't need to impress people they don't like. Success is not found in achieving what you aim at but in aiming at what you ought to achieve.

> *Happy is the man who doesn't give in and do wrong when he is tempted, for afterwards he will get as his reward the crown of life that God has promised those who love him.*
>
> —JAMES 1:12 TLB

Perfection, fortunately, is not the best alternative to mediocrity. A more sensible alternative is excellence. Striving for excellence rather than perfection is stimulating and rewarding; striving for perfection in practically anything is frustrating and futile. Paul says,

> *I advise you to obey only the Holy Spirit's instructions. He will tell you where to go and what to do, and then you won't always be doing the wrong things your evil nature wants you to.*
>
> —GALATIANS 5:16 TLB

Human excellence means nothing unless it works with the consent and power of God.

There is always a heavy demand for fresh mediocrity—don't give in to it. Instead, be easily satisfied with the very best. When you are delivering your very best is when you will feel most successful. Ted Engstrom clarifies, "Excellence demands that you be better than yourself." Never sell your principles for popularity or you'll find yourself bankrupt in the worst way. Dare to be true to the best you know.

Opportunities Hide
Behind Obstacles

T HE UNITED STATES STANDARD RAILROAD gauge (distance between the rails) is 4 feet, 8.5 inches. That's an exceedingly odd number. Why was that gauge used? Because that's the way they built them in England, and English expatriates built U.S. railroads. Why did the English build them like that? Because the first rail lines were built by the same people who built the pre-railroad tramways, and that's the gauge they used.

Why did "they" use that gauge, then? Because the people who built the tramways used the same jigs and tools that they used for building wagons, which used that wheel spacing. Okay! Why did the wagons have that particular odd wheel spacing? Well, if they tried to use any other spacing, the wagon wheels would break on some of the old, long-distance English roads, because that's the spacing of the wheel ruts.

So who built those old rutted roads? The first long-distance roads in Europe (and England) were built by the Romans for their imperial legions. The roads have been used ever since. And the ruts? Roman chariots made the initial ruts, which everyone else had to match for fear of destroying their wagons and wheels.

Since the chariots were made for (and/or by) the Roman empire, they were all alike in the matter of wheel spacing.

Thus, we have the answer to our original question. The United States' standard railroad gauge of 4 feet, 8.5 inches derives from the original specification for an imperial Roman war chariot. But why did the Romans use that spacing? Their chariots were made just wide enough to accommodate the back ends of two war-horses.

And now, the twist to the tale . . .

There's an interesting extension to the story about railroad gauges and horses' behinds. When we see a space shuttle sitting on its launch pad, there are two big boosters attached to the sides of the main fuel tank. These are solid rocket boosters, or SRBs.

Thiokol makes the SRBs at its factory in Utah. The engineers who designed the SRBs might have preferred to make them a bit fatter, but the SRBs had to be shipped by train from the factory to the launch site. The railroad line from the factory had to run through a tunnel in the mountains. The SRBs had to fit through that tunnel. The tunnel is slightly wider than the railroad track, and the railroad track is about as wide as two horses' behinds.

So, the major design feature of what is arguably the world's most advanced transportation system was determined by the width of a horse's rear end (from Internet humor archives).

Obstacles are a part of life and many times lead to excellent opportunities. Not all obstacles are bad. In fact, an opportunity's favorite disguise is an obstacle. You will always meet obstacles on the road to your answer. The fight is good; it is proof that you haven't quit and are still alive.

No one is immune to problems. Even the lion has to fight off flies. The apostle Paul said it best:

We are pressed on every side by troubles, but not crushed and broken. We are perplexed because we don't know why things happen as they do, but we don't give up and quit. We are hunted down, but God never abandons us. We get knocked down, but we get up again and keep going.

—2 CORINTHIANS 4:8–9 TLB

Being a diligent person does not remove you from the world and its problems; rather, it positions you to live in it productively and victoriously. Thomas Carlyle said, "The block of granite that was an obstacle in the pathway of the weak becomes a stepping-stone in the pathway of the strong."

Good news! In the midst of every trial, there is growth and promotion for you. Each challenge provides an opportunity to grow, not die.

Obstacles can temporarily detour you, but only *you* can make *you* stop. Your struggle may be lasting, but it is not everlasting. It's wrong to think that there's nothing more permanent than this temporary situation.

Obstacles will reveal what you truly believe and who you really are. They introduce you to yourself. You will find out what you honestly believe in the face of a problem.

As I've traveled, I've noticed that no matter how cloudy it is when the plane takes off, above the clouds the sun always shines. Look up! It's not the "out look" but the "up look" that counts.

Your life will be much more productive if you understand that obstacles are a part of life. If you want your place in the sun, you'll have to expect some blisters. Studs Terkel said, "Face the music, and someday you may lead the band." The difference between iron and steel is fire, and the fire-tried steel is worth it.

INVENT OR IMPROVE

ALL PROGRESS IS DUE to those who were not satisfied to let well enough alone. "Acorns were good until bread was found," said Francis Bacon. The majority fails because of its lack of persistence in creating new plans to improve the ones that succeed.

If you can't think up a new idea, find a way to make better use of an old one. "Where we cannot invent, we may at least improve," said Charles Caleb Colton.

Don't look for the answer to your problem; look for many answers, then choose the best one. Do more than is required and continue doing it. "The difference between ordinary and extraordinary is that little extra," says Zig Ziglar.

There is always a way—then there is always a better way. When you've found something—look again. School is never out! The more you truly desire something, the more you will try to find a better way.

The biggest enemy of best is good. If you're satisfied with what's good, you'll never have what's best.

It's what you learn after you know it all that counts.

—JOHN WOODEN

The man who thinks he knows it all has merely stopped thinking. If you think you've arrived, you'll be left behind. A successful man continues to look for work after he has found a job.

Take the offensive. Cause something to happen. Don't waste time defending your present position. Create a habit of taking the initiative and don't ever start your day in neutral. Don't leave well enough alone. If at first you do succeed, try something harder.

> *Show me a thoroughly satisfied man, and I will show you a failure.*
>
> —THOMAS EDISON

"There are two kinds of men who never amount to very much," Cyrus H. K. Curtis remarked to his associate, Edward Bok.

"And what kinds are those?" inquired Bok.

"Those who cannot do what they are told," replied the famous publisher, "and those who can do nothing else."

Find a better way, and make that way better.

CRITICISM IS A COMPLIMENT WHEN YOU'RE DOING THE RIGHT THING

A WOMAN ACCOMPANIED HER HUSBAND to the doctor. After his checkup, the doctor called the wife into his office alone. He said, "Your husband is suffering from a severe disease, combined with horrible stress. If you don't do the following, your husband will surely die: Each morning fix him a healthy breakfast. Be pleasant and make sure he is in a good mood. For lunch make him a nutritious meal. For dinner prepare an especially nice meal for him. Don't burden him with chores, as he probably has had a hard day. Don't discuss your problems with him; it will only make his stress worse. And most important, satisfy his every whim. If you can do this for the next ten months to a year, I think your husband will regain his health completely."

On the way home, the husband asked his wife, "What did the doctor say?"

"You're going to die," she replied.

Have you ever felt this way after being around some people? Do you feel worse? Do you want to give up?

All great ideas create conflict. In other words, what you

want to do in life will create challenges and criticism. Decide today: I will not surrender my dream to noisy negatives.

It seems that every great idea has this order of responses:

(1) "It's impossible—don't waste the time and money."
(2) "It's possible but has a limited value."
(3) "I said all along it was a good idea."

Foes and critics are never interested in solving the problem, and they never offer a better solution. They are like an armless man who teaches others to throw.

If your head sticks up above the crowd, expect more criticism than applause. Have you noticed that no one ever erects a statue of a critic?

Whoever criticizes others *to* you will criticize *you* to others. If someone belittles you, he is only trying to cut you down to his size. While throwing mud, critics are simultaneously losing ground.

You can always tell a failure by the way he criticizes success. Those who can, do. Those who can't, criticize. Those who complain about the way the ball bounces are usually the ones who dropped it.

Sticks and stones are only thrown at fruit-bearing trees. If it were not for the doers, the critics would soon be out of business. Envy provides the mud that failures throw at success. Kenneth Tynan put it in these words:

A critic is a man who thinks he knows the way but can't drive the car.

Small minds are the first to condemn great ideas.

If people talk negatively about you, live and work so that

no one will believe them. Fear of criticism is the kiss of death in the courtship of achievement.

The only way to eliminate criticism is to do nothing and be nothing. If you are afraid of criticism, you won't accomplish much. A successful man is one who can lay a firm foundation with the bricks that others throw at him.

Envy Grabs at Others and Steals From Itself

PICTURE A RUNNER in full stride. He speeds through a pack of contenders, but he begins to look at whom he's running against. What is the inevitable conclusion to this scene? That runner will slow down and probably stumble. The same will happen to us if we allow the distraction of envy to turn our head as we run the race set before us. Instead of breaking records, we'll break our momentum.

"The man who covets is always poor" (Claudian). Envy never enriched any man.

> *Of all the passions, jealousy is that which exacts the hardest service and pays the bitterest wages. Its service is to watch the success of our enemy; its wages, to be sure of it.*
>
> —CHARLES CALEB COLTON

Envy is like biting a dog because the dog bit you. Here's an accurate description of its self-punishment: "Envy shoots at others and wounds herself" (English maxim). Proverbs counsels, "A relaxed attitude lengthens a man's life; jealousy rots it away" (14:30 TLB). Like rust consumes iron, envy consumes itself.

Envy drains the joy, satisfaction, and purpose out of living. If allowed to grow, it breeds hatred and revenge. Revenge converts a little right into a big wrong. Watch out! It's an appetite that's never satisfied.

"It is not love that is blind, but jealousy" (Lawrence Durrell). Envy sees the sea but not the rocks.

> *When an envious man hears another praised, he feels himself injured.*
>
> —ENGLISH PROVERB

Josh Billings muses, "Love looks through a telescope, envy through a microscope." We underrate or exaggerate that which we don't possess. Your life is too valuable to waste through wanting what others have.

Some people seem to know how to live everybody's lives but their own. Envy is the consuming desire to have everyone else a little less successful than youself. Don't measure your success by what others have or haven't done. In other words, don't try to get even with your enemies and ahead of your friends.

Envy is a tremendous waste of mental energy. Refrain from envy, or it will be the root of most of your unhappiness. Covetousness is the tribute mediocrity pays to achievers.

A person is wise when he doesn't long for the things he doesn't have but is instead thankful for those things he does have. Continually compare what you want with what you have, and you'll be unhappy. Instead, compare what you deserve with what you have, and you'll be ecstatic. Decide to stick with appreciation. Envy is too great a burden to bear.

REAL WINNERS KEEP ON WINNING

HOW MANY PEOPLE of great potential have you known? Where did they all go? If people of great potential stop, it's because they don't build on their victories. There are two distinct times when a person is most likely to quit: after a mistake, and after a victory. Success has made failures of many people.

Once you're moving, you can keep moving. Did Michael Jordan stop shooting after making his first bucket? Did John Grisham quit writing after his first bestseller? Successful people know that each victory buys an admission ticket to a more challenging opportunity.

One of the greatest benefits of success is the opportunity to do more. John Wicker noted, "Opportunities multiply as they are seized. They die when neglected. Life is a long line of opportunities." The more you do, the more you can do.

Perhaps it is a good thing that you haven't seen all your dreams come true. For when you get all you wish for, you will be miserable. To be forever reaching out, to remain unsatisfied is a key to momentum.

—NORTH CAROLINA CHRISTIAN ADVOCATE

I'm not suggesting that you don't stop and smell the roses along the journey. Just don't stay so long past the victory of the blossom that the petals have dropped, the limbs have been pruned, and all that's left are the thorns.

The first step toward going somewhere significant is deciding that you're not going to stay where you are. When you have a victory, comfort and money will follow, but don't confuse comfort with joy or money with success.

It's not what you get that makes you successful; rather, it is what you are continuing to do with what you've got that measures your success. Once again, the person who is satisfied with what he has done will never become famous for what he will do.

Remember this your lifetime through—
Tomorrow there will be more to do.
Failure waits for all those who stay
With some success made yesterday.

—ANONYMOUS

ENTHUSIASM IS AN INSIDE JOB

M Y WIFE AND I DECIDED to have a cup of coffee at the local International House of Pancakes. Inside, we were greeted by a friendly, happy, smiling waitress. It didn't take us long to notice that she had only one tooth. On the top and in the middle. I thought, *Isn't that interesting? Here's a woman with one tooth, yet she works in a job that requires a lot of up-close people contact. She's smiling, and doing a good job.*

Then I noticed a button she was wearing: "A smile is a gift you can give every day." What a profound scene this was. So much so that I complimented her on her button and sincerely told her she had a nice smile. I wondered if anyone had ever told her that.

When she returned to our table she told me that her father had done the calligraphy on the button. She said, "He had his fingers cut off in an industrial accident and then decided to pick up calligraphy *after that!*" In fact, his writing was better now than before the tragedy.

Perhaps only a woman raised by a fingerless dad who does calligraphy can choose to smile even though she has only one tooth.

Enthusiasm makes everything different. You can't control the length of each day, but you can control its impact by adding fun and enthusiasm. When you have enthusiasm for life, life has enthusiasm for you.

William Ward said, "Enthusiasm and persistence can make an average person superior; indifference and lethargy can make a superior person average." Don't postpone joy. Instead, be like the Mona Lisa—she keeps smiling when her back's to the wall.

If you find yourself dog-tired at night, it may be because you growled all day. Learn to laugh at yourself. A person with a great sense of humor may bore others, but he rarely has a dull moment himself.

> *Of all the things God created, I am often most grateful He created laughter.*
>
> —CHUCK SWINDOLL

Humor is to life what shock absorbers are to automobiles. Thank God for them on bumpy roads!

One of the single most powerful things you can do to have influence over others is to smile at them. You are never fully dressed until you wear a smile. It's the best face-lift!

A smile is an asset; a frown is a liability. Some people grin and bear it; others smile and change it. Smiling—being happy and enthusiastic—is always a choice, not a result. It improves your personality and others' opinion of you.

Both enthusiasm and pessimism are contagious. How much of each do you spread? Our attitudes tell others what we expect in return. A laugh a day keeps the negative away.

> *It's difficult to remain neutral or indifferent in the presence of a positive thinker.*
>
> —DENIS WAITLEY

You can succeed at almost anything for which you have

unlimited enthusiasm. "In my experience, the best creative work is never done when one is unhappy," said Albert Einstein.

Enthusiasm gives you the proper perspective on life. Helen Keller suggested, "Keep your face to the sunshine, and you cannot see the shadow." A smile is a powerful, positive weapon with which to attack life.

Every significant success is accomplished with enthusiasm. For every opportunity you miss because you're too enthusiastic, you will miss a hundred because you're not enthusiastic enough. You will rarely succeed at anything unless you have fun doing it.

FEAR IS FAITH IN REVERSE

The worst liars in the world are your own fears:
Worry is the traitor in our camp that dampens our
powder and weakens our aim.

—WILLIAM JORDEN

William Ward showed the difference between faith and worry:

Worry is faith in the negative, trust in the unpleasant,
assurance of disaster and belief in defeat. . . . Worry is
a magnet that attracts negative conditions. Faith is a
more powerful force that creates positive circum-
stances. . . . Worry is wasting today's time to clutter
up tomorrow's opportunities with yesterday's troubles.

What causes most battles to be lost is unfounded fear of the enemy's strength. A. Purnell Bailey says worry is like a fog:

The Bureau of Standards in Washington tells us that a dense fog covering seven city blocks, one hundred feet deep, is comprised of something less than one glass of water. That amount of water is divided into some 60,000,000 tiny drops. Not much there! Yet when these minute particles settle down over the city or countryside, they can blot out practically all vision. A cup full of worry does just about the same thing. The tiny drops of fretfulness close around our thoughts and we are submerged without vision.

Dale Carnegie wrote, "An old man was asked what had robbed him of joy in his life. His reply was 'Things that never happened.'" Fear wants you to run from things that aren't after you. It's never safe to look into the future with eyes of fear.

Do you remember the things you were worrying about a year ago? How did they work out? Didn't you waste a lot of energy on account of most of them? Didn't most of them turn out to be fine after all? Almost 99 percent of the things that we worry about don't happen. Fear is a poor chisel to carve out your tomorrows.

I follow this famous advice: "At night, I give all my worries and fears to God. He's going to be up all night anyway." Peter puts it like this:

Let him have all your worries and cares, for he is always thinking about you and watching everything that concerns you.

—1 Peter 5:7 tlb

Never make a decision based on fear. Don't ever find yourself giving something the "benefit of the doubt"—doubt has no benefit. One of the great discoveries you can make is to find that you can do what you were afraid you couldn't do.

Go Out on a Limb—That's Where the Fruit Is

MOSES AND THE PEOPLE were in the desert, but what was he going to do with them? They had to be fed, and feed them is what he did, according to the quartermaster general in the Army. It is reported that Moses would have to have provided 1,500 tons of food each day.

To bring that much food each day, two freight trains—each a mile long—would be required! Besides, you must remember that they were out in the desert, so they would need firewood for cooking. This would take 4,000 tons of wood and a few more freight trains—each a mile long—just for one day.

And just think: they were forty years in transit. They would have to have water. If they only had enough to drink and wash a few dishes, it would take 11,000,000 gallons each day, and a freight train with tank cars—1,800 miles long—just to bring it!

But then, there is another problem. Each time they settled at the end of the day, a campground two-thirds the size of Rhode Island was required: 750 square miles.

Do you think Moses figured all this out before he left Egypt?

I think not! You see, Moses trusted God. God took care of these things for him. Do you really think God has any problem taking care of all your needs?

Too many people expect little, ask for little, receive little, and are content with little. Having a dream is not trying to believe something regardless of the evidence; dreaming is daring to do something regardless of the consequences. I sincerely believe that every one of us would accomplish far more if we did not automatically view achievements as impossibilities.

> *Don't wait for all the lights to be green before you leave the house.*
>
> —JIM STOVALL

Don't ever say that conditions aren't perfect; this will always limit you. If you wait for conditions to be exactly right, you will never do anything. Wayne Gretzky is probably the greatest hockey player in history. Asked about his secret for continuing to lead the NHL in scoring year after year, he replied,

> *I skate to where the puck is going to be, not where it has been.*

Those who dare, do; those who dare not, do not. Don't do anything that doesn't require vision. Isak Dinesen said, "God made the world round so that we would never be able to see too far down the road." Once again, the person who dares for nothing need hope for nothing.

I really believe the best way to live your life is outside the box. The future belongs to those who can think original thoughts, see where no one is looking, and take action before it's obvious.

Let your faith run ahead of your mind. Go farther than you

can see. Significant achievements have never been obtained by taking small risks on unimportant issues.

> *If you're hunting rabbits in tiger country, you must keep your eye peeled for tigers, but when you are hunting tigers you can ignore the rabbits.*
>
> —HENRY STERN

Don't be distracted by the rabbits. Set your sights on "big game."

You have reached stagnation when all you ever exercise is caution. Sometimes you must press ahead despite the pounding fear in your head that says, "Turn back."

> *Our destiny says to us,*
> *"Come to the edge."*
> *We say, "It's too high."*
> *"Come to the edge."*
> *We say, "I might fall."*
> *"Come to the edge," Destiny says.*
> *And we stepped out.*
> *And it pushed us.*
> *And we flew.*
>
> —PARAPHRASE OF POEM BY APOLLINAIRE

PASSION IS POWERFUL

E VERY PERSON HAS THE POTENTIAL to be passionate. Everyone loves something. We are shaped and motivated by what we love. It reveals our passion. Enthusiasm is a
choice, not a result.

Ignore what you are passionate about, and you ignore one
of the greatest potentials inside you. Nothing significant was
ever achieved without passion. Keep following this success
principle from Ecclesiastes: "Whatever your hand finds to do,
do it with all your might" (9:10).

Most winners are ex-losers who got passionate. The worst
bankruptcy in the world is the person who has lost his enthusiasm, his passion. When you add passion to a belief, it
becomes a conviction. Conviction gets more done than belief
ever dreamed.

The starting point of all accomplishment is desire. Keep
this in mind: Feeble desires bring feeble results, just as a small
amount of fire makes a small amount of heat. Be passionate
about your life. Act from your passions. The more energy you
apply to any task, the more you will have to apply to the next
task.

Desire is like planting a seed. It causes something to begin to grow. Deep desire creates not only its own opportunities, but its own talents. Attitudes alter abilities.

It's passion that persuades.

> *A strong passion for any object will insure success, for the desire of the end will point out the means.*
> —WILLIAM HAZLITT

The trouble with many educated men is that learning goes to their heads and not to their hearts. Does the path you're traveling capture your heart? You have been sent into this world to do something into which you can pour your heart.

You will be remembered in life only for your passions. Find something that consumes you. A belief is not just an idea a person possesses; it is an idea that possesses a person. Learn to be comfortable with being enthusiastic.

Every time zeal and passion are discussed, someone brings up *balance*. Balance itself is a tremendous virtue, but its immediate neighbors are apathy and weakness. If the truth were known, "being balanced" is usually an excuse for being lukewarm, indifferent, or neutral ... three traits that are always attached to failure.

Enthusiasm can achieve in one day what it takes centuries to achieve by reason. Proverbs says,

> *Above all else, guard your affections. For they influence everything else in your life. (14:23* TLB*)*

William James said, "Perhaps the greatest discovery of this century is that if you change your attitude, you can change your life."

Put a smile on what you do. It adds to your face value.

When your enthusiasm increases, stress and fear in your life diminish. Passion is powerful.

When you're driven by passionate conviction, you can do anything you want with your life—except give up on the thing you care about. Pessimism never wins. Mike Murdock said, "What generates passion and zeal in you is a clue to revealing your destiny. What you love is a clue to something you contain."

Life is a passion, or it is nothing:

Without passion man is a mere latent force and a possibility, like the flint that awaits the shock of the iron before it can give forth its spark.
—HENRI FREDERIC AMIEL

Passion is the spark for your fuse. In fact, the bigger the challenge or opportunity, the more enthusiasm is required. Follow this advice for a successful life:

There are many things that will catch my eye, but there are only a very few that catch my heart. . . . It is those I consider to pursue.
—TIM REDMOND

As Terrence Deal sagely notes, "Believing is seeing. It's much more effective than the old notion that seeing is believing." If you have the right desire, the distance doesn't matter. Love the thing you do, and you will keep doing better and bigger things.

THERE IS SIMPLY MORE TO LIFE THAN INCREASING ITS SPEED

BEVERLY SILLS SAYS, "There are no shortcuts to any place worth going." The way to the top is neither swift nor easy. Nothing worthwhile ever happens in a hurry—so be patient. Because of impatience, we are driven too soon from what we're supposed to do. Don't be impatient: remember, you can't warm your hands by burning your fingers.

Your success has less to do with speed and more to do with timing and direction. The key is doing the right thing at the right time. Tyron Edwards said, "Have a time and place for everything, and do everything in its time and place, and you will not only accomplish more, but have far more leisure than those who are always hurrying." The problem is that many a go-getter never stops long enough to let opportunity catch up with him.

> *Whoever is in a hurry shows that the thing he is about is too big for him.*
>
> —LORD CHESTERFIELD

When you are outside of the right timing, you will sow hurry and reap frustration. What benefit is running if you're on the wrong road?

Brendan Francis commented, "Failure at a task may be the result of having tackled it at the wrong time." If the time has passed, preparation does no good. The trouble with life in the fast lane is that you get to the other end too soon. Søren Kierkegaard said, "Most men pursue pleasure with such breathless haste that they hurry past it." Haste makes waste; give time, time. Many people overestimate what they can do in a year and underestimate what they can do in a lifetime.

> *There is no road too long to the man who advances deliberately and without undue haste; no honor is too distant to the man who prepares himself for it with patience.*
>
> —JEAN DE LA BRUYERE

Many times the action you take at the right time has no immediate relationship to the answer—it's merely to get you to the right place at the right time.

We are happiest when we discover that what we should be doing and what we are doing are the same thing. Ecclesiastes affirms, "To every thing there is a season, and a time to every purpose under the heaven" (3:1 KJV). You will never be what you ought to be until you are doing what you ought to be doing.

If you are facing the right direction, just keep on walking.

> *The lame man who keeps the right road outstrips the runner who takes a wrong one.... The more active and swift the latter is the further he will go astray.*
>
> —FRANCIS BACON

Determine to choose the right pace: If you go too quickly, you can catch up with misfortune, and if you go too slowly, misfortune can catch up with you. When you are both patient and persistent, you miss the wrong places and end up where you're supposed to be.

OPPORTUNITIES ARE EVERYWHERE YOU ARE

SOMETIMES AS I DRIVE DOWN different parts of my city, I can't help but notice the vast variety of businesses. Many times I pause and think, "That's someone's dream; that's someone's unique idea; that's someone's million-dollar opportunity." I believe there are significant opportunities and ideas around us every day. In fact,

> *God hides things by putting them near us.*
> —RALPH WALDO EMERSON

The best opportunities and ideas are hidden near you, but you must be on the lookout for them. You can see a thousand opportunities around you every day . . . or you can see nothing. Your big opportunity may be right where you are now.

Too many people spend their whole lives devoted to only solving problems and not recognizing opportunities. Significant growth always comes from building on talents, gifts, and strengths, not by solving problems. Where do you hear opportunity knocking? How can you answer that knock? "There are always opportunities everywhere, just as there always have been" (Charles Fillmore).

You can find opportunities close at hand by paying more attention to the things that are working positively in your life than to those that are giving you trouble. Too many times people devote the majority of their effort, time, and attention to endeavors that are never going to be productive. Clear your mind of the things that are out of your control so you can focus and act upon what you can control. One of life's greatest tragedies is to lose an opportunity and not realize it.

> *You are, at this moment, standing right in the middle of your own "acres of diamonds."*
>
> —EARL NIGHTINGALE

At any given moment you have more possibility than you can act upon. There are million-dollar opportunities around you every day. I agree with *Pogo*'s insight:

> *Gentlemen, we're surrounded by insurmountable opportunities.*

"The successful person always has a number of projects planned, to which he looks forward. Any one of them could change the course of his life overnight" (Mark Caine). Opportunities? They are all around us. There are opportunities lying dormant everywhere, waiting for the observant eye to discover them.

Earl Nightingale said, "Wherever there is danger, there lurks opportunity; wherever there is opportunity, there lurks danger. The two are inseparable. They go together." For example, stars are constantly shining, but we usually don't see them until night's darkest hours. The same is true with opportunities. Problems are opportunities, and there are more than we can count.

Forgive Them—It's the Last Thing Your Enemies Want You to Do

AS NOTED EARLIER, forgiveness is the key to personal peace; it releases action and creates freedom. We all need to say the right thing after doing the wrong thing. Josiah Bailey affirms, "It is the truth that those who forgive most shall be most forgiven."

One of the secrets of a long and fruitful life is to forgive everybody everything every night before you go to bed. When you have a huge chip on your shoulder, it causes you to lose your balance. If you would quit nursing a grudge, it would die. You don't need a doctor to tell you it's better to remove a grudge than to nurse it. There's nothing heavier that you can place on your own shoulders.

It is far better to forgive and forget than to hate and remember. Again, Josh Billings says, "There is no revenge so complete as forgiveness." *Unforgiveness blocks blessings; forgiveness releases blessings.* Why aren't some prayers answered? D. L. Moody addressed this: "I firmly believe that a great many prayers are not answered because we are not willing to forgive someone."

Do you want to release the past and claim the future? Forgiveness doesn't erase the former, but it does enhance the latter. Harry Emerson Fosdick said, "No one can be wrong with man and right with God." You can be wrong in the middle of being right when you don't forgive.

Paul says in Ephesians,

Let all bitterness, wrath, and anger, and clamour, and evil speaking, be put away from you, with all malice; and be ye kind to one another, tenderhearted, forgiving one another, even as God for Christ's sake hath forgiven you. (4:31–32 KJV)

Ask yourself: If God is willing to forgive, then who am I to hold out?

Are You Trying to Go Somewhere in Neutral?

L ET ME ASK YOU the age-old question: "Are you waiting on God, or is He waiting on you?" I believe the vast majority of time, He is waiting on us. Is God your hope, or is He your excuse? I'm convinced He wants you to take the initiative, to live your life on the offensive. William Menninger said,

> *The amount of satisfaction you get from life depends largely on your own ingenuity, self-sufficiency, and resourcefulness. People who wait around for life to supply their satisfaction usually find boredom instead.*

Albert Hubert remarked, "[People] who want milk should not seat themselves on a stool in the middle of the field and hope that the cow will back up to them." The door of opportunity won't open unless you push. Don't sit back and take what comes. Go after what you want.

Being on the defensive has never produced ultimate victory. I believe that God helps the courageous. Follow Sara Teasdale's lead:

I make the most of all that comes and the least of all that goes.

E. M. Bounds said,

There is neither [biblical] encouragement nor room . . . for feeble desires, listless efforts, lazy atti-tudes; all must be strenuous, urgent, ardent. Flamed desires, impassioned, unwearied insistence delights heaven. God would have His children incorrigibly in earnest and persistently bold in their efforts.

When you are bold, His mighty powers will come to your aid.

Get aggressive and go after opportunities. They usually don't find you—you must find them. The reason most people don't go very far in life is that they sidestep opportunity and shake hands with procrastination. Procrastination is the grave in which opportunity is buried. Don't be out in the backyard looking for four-leaf clovers when opportunity knocks at your front door.

For the tenacious there is always time and opportunity. Francis Bacon observed, "A wise man will make more oppor-tunities than he finds." Are you waiting on opportunities, or are opportunities waiting on you? Take the initiative and live your life on the offensive.

It's more valuable to find a situation that redistributes opportunity than one that redistributes money. Have you ever noticed that great people never lack opportunities? When suc-cessful people are interviewed, they always mention their big plans for the future. Observing them, most people would think, "If I were in their shoes, I'd kick back and do nothing." *Success should not diminish desire. If it does, it won't remain successful.*

Helen Keller said, "Never bend your head. Hold it high.

Look the world straight in the eyes." If you want success you must seize your own opportunities as you go. I agree with Jonathan Winters:

> *I couldn't wait for success—so I went ahead without it.*

Lillian Hellman said, "It is best to act with confidence, no matter how little right you have to it." It is always a bumpy, uphill road that leads to heights of greatness.

George Adams said, "In this life we only get those things for which we hunt, for which we strive and for which we are willing to sacrifice." Don't just face opportunities and problems; attack them. Consider the insight of B. C. Forbes: "Mediocre men wait for opportunities to come to them. Strong, able, alert men go after opportunity."

There is far more opportunity than ability. Life is full of golden opportunities. Every person has a lot that he or she can do. Start with what you can do; don't stop because of what you can't do. Great opportunities will come as you make the most of small ones. Many people seem to think that opportunity means a chance to get money without earning it. The best gifts we get are opportunities, not things. Seize them!

I Dare You to Live by Faith

DON'T DO ANYTHING THAT doesn't require faith. The key to momentum is always having something in faith to look forward to, something to anticipate. We live by faith or we don't live at all. Either we venture or we vegetate. Needed: more people who specialize in the impossible! This year's success was last year's impossibility.

> *Faith is not trying to believe something regardless of the evidence. Faith is daring to do something regardless of the consequence.*
>
> —SHERWOOD EDDY

"Do not pray for easy lives. Pray to be stronger men. Do not pray for tasks equal to your power. Pray for power equal to your tasks" (Phillips Brooks). Jesus said to us, "I [have] come that they might have life, and that they might have it more abundantly" (John 10:10 KJV). Never be afraid to do what God tells you to do. Again, Les Brown advised, "Shoot for the moon. Even if you miss it, you will land among the stars."

You can only accomplish in proportion to what you attempt. The reason why so little is accomplished is generally because so little is attempted. Remember: Never say never. You have to think big to be big. What is "the impossible"? The impossible is what nobody can do until somebody does.

You do not tap the resources of God until you attempt the impossible. Risk is part of God's plan. "I can do everything God asks me to do with the help of Christ who gives me the strength and power" (Philippians 4:13 TLB). Even a coward can praise Christ, but it takes a man of courage to follow Him.

To review: Progress always involves risk. You can't steal second base if your foot is still on first. He who does not dare will not get his share. Unless you enter the beehive, you cannot take the honey. A great ship always asks for deep water. When you dare for nothing, you should hope for nothing. God wants us to bite off more than we can chew, to live by faith and not by sight.

To Compare Is Never Fair

NEVER MEASURE YOUR SUCCESS by what others have or haven't done. It's never fair to compare. People are either a voice or an echo, a thermometer or a thermostat. I agree with Pat Riley: "Don't let other people tell you what you want." Jacqueline Briskin warns, "Don't take anybody else's definition of success as your own."

No one can build a personal destiny upon the faith or experience of another person. The old saying is true,

You have to do your own growing, no matter how tall your grandfather is.

You will find that successful people's main concern is rarely what others are thinking. However, people would worry less about what others think about them if they only realized how seldom they do. They're usually not thinking about you but wondering what you're thinking about them. I believe that God rarely uses a person whose main concern is what others are thinking. In fact, judging and comparing yourself to others is a profound waste of energy. This thinking halts progress and inhibits your forward motion.

If you think you're doing better than the average person, you're an average person. Why would you want to compare yourself with someone average? Too many people seem to know how to live everybody's life but their own. We need to stop comparing ourselves to others.

Cynthia Kersey says, "Consider this strategy for success:

(1) Consult management; if they hate the idea, proceed with it. If they like the idea, reconsider.

(2) Hire market researchers. If they say the idea will fail, assume it will succeed.

(3) Never ask how much your idea will cost, and don't worry about how much it will make.

(4) When everyone you know—colleagues, partners, friends, and family—says the idea is crazy, then plow ahead, because you've got a sure hit on your hands."

This was apparently the strategy of a high school dropout, an admittedly mediocre artist with almost no business sense, who founded the greatest entertainment empire in history: His name was Walt Disney.

Once again, "Every man must do two things alone. He must do his own believing and his own dying" (Martin Luther). When you compare yourself with others, you will become either bitter or vain, for there will always be greater and lesser persons than you. Making comparisons is a sure path to frustration, and comparison is never proof of anything.

What a squandering of resources to compare your place and plan with that of other people! What happens in another person's life has no impact and no effect on what happens in yours. I was amazed recently when I heard from a friend I hadn't talked with in three or four years. He told me that he felt bad for his life because of some of the success that had happened in mine. I couldn't help but be perplexed at his comments, and I responded to him by asking, "Do you mean that you would have felt a lot better if I'd done horribly the last three or four years?" Well, of course he said no. It just points out the mutually exclusive facts: What's happening in another person's life is no basis for how well or how badly you're doing in your own.

Life is more fun when you don't keep score for others. When you compare your place and plan with that of others, you really are insisting on running someone else's life. Success is simply a matter of doing what *you* do best and not worrying about what the other person is going to do. You carry success or failure within yourself—it doesn't depend on outside conditions.

Ask yourself the question posed by Earl Nightingale: "Are you motivated by what you really want out of life, or are you mass-motivated?" Make sure you decide what you really want, not what someone else wants for you. Do you say, "I'm good, but not as good as I ought to be" or do you say, "I'm not as bad as a lot of other people"? The longer you dwell on another's weakness, the more you affect your own mind with unhappiness. You must create your own system, your own plan, or be enslaved by someone else's. Don't compare—your purpose is to create!

If a thousand people say something foolish, it's still foolish. Direction from God is never a matter of the consensus of public opinion. A wise man makes his own decision; an ignorant man follows the majority. Don't think you're necessarily on the right road because it's a well-beaten path. The greatest risk in life is to wait for and depend on others for your security.

"We only become what we are by the radical and deep-seated refusal of that which others have made of us" (Jean-Paul

Sartre). Every person who trims himself to suit everybody will soon find himself whittled away. Therefore, don't compare your place or plan with that of others. Compare your place and plan with God's will and His Word for your life.

Knowledge Doesn't Speak Loudly

T HERE WAS A YOUNG LADY who had to do a lot of flying for her business. It made her very, very nervous, so she always took her Bible along—reading it helped her to relax on the long flights.

One time she was sitting next to a businessman. When he saw her pull out the Bible, he gave a little chuckle and a smirk and went back to what he was doing.

After a while he turned to her and asked, "You don't really believe all that stuff in there, do you?"

The lady replied, "Of course I do. It's the Bible."

He said, "Well, what about that guy that was swallowed by that whale?"

She replied, "Oh, Jonah. Yes, I believe that; it's in the Bible."

He asked, "Well, how do you suppose he survived all that time inside the whale?"

The lady said, "Well, I don't really know. I guess when I get to heaven, I'll ask him."

"What if he isn't in heaven?" the man asked sarcastically.

"Then you can ask him," replied the lady.

"Keep your mouth closed and you'll stay out of trouble" (Proverbs 21:23 TLB). What great advice! A man is known by the silence he keeps. Don't miss many valuable opportunities to hold your tongue and listen to what the other person is saying. When you have nothing to say, say nothing. Silence is a friend who will never betray you.

One of the best ways to persuade others is by listening to them. You'll find that a gossip talks to you about others, a bore talks to you about himself, and a brilliant conversationalist talks to you about yourself and listens to what you say. You don't learn anything while you're talking. The truth is that the more you say, the less people remember. When it comes to talking, it's always more blessed to receive than to give.

The greatest skill you can develop is the skill of listening to others. The second greatest skill you can develop is getting others to listen to you.

The man of few words and settled mind is wise; therefore, even a fool is thought to be wise when he is silent. It pays him to keep his mouth shut.
—Proverbs 17:27–28 TLB

Talk is cheap because supply exceeds demand. "As you go through life, you are going to have many opportunities to keep your mouth shut. Take advantage of all of them" (*West Virginia Gazette*). There must have been some reason God made our ears to stay open and our mouth to close. *As a man grows older and wiser, he talks less and says more.*

Learn to listen. Sometimes opportunity disguises itself this way and knocks very softly. You will find that God will speak for the man who holds his peace. Too much talk will always include error. There is only one rule for being a good talker: Learn to listen. Be a good listener; your ears will never get you in trouble. One of the most powerful principles you can implement in your life is that of listening to others. Proverbs 10:19: "Don't talk so much. You keep putting your foot in your mouth. Be sensible and turn off the flow!" (TLB).

WHAT FORCE IS MORE POTENT THAN LOVE?

—Igor Stravinsky

LOVE IS THE MOST IMPORTANT ingredient of success; without it, your life will echo with emptiness. Jesus said, "By this shall all men know that ye are my disciples, if you have love one to another" (John 13:35 KJV). There is a simple way to live a life of love. Breathe in God's Spirit, and you'll exhale His love.

We are all born for love. It's easy to hate; it's difficult to love. Good things are difficult to achieve, and bad things are easy to get. Love will find a way—everything else will find an excuse. "Let love be your greatest aim" (1 Corinthians 14:1 TLB).

Kindness has converted more sinners than zeal, eloquence, or learning. Love people more than they deserve. Never lose a chance to say a kind word to another person. Henry Drummond said, "You will find as you look back upon your life that the moments when you have really lived are the moments when you have done things in a spirit of love." Love opens doors and removes limitations:

*Constant kindness can accomplish much. As the sun
makes ice melt, kindness causes misunderstanding,
mistrust and hostility to evaporate.*

—ALBERT SCHWEITZER

Practice constant kindness.

To be loved, be lovable. Make it a point to love someone
who doesn't deserve it. THE MESSAGE translation says,

*Most of all, love each other as if your life depended on
it. Love makes up for practically anything.*

—1 PETER 4:8

"What does love look like? It has the hands to help others.
It has the feet to hasten to the poor and needy. It has the eyes
to see misery and want. It has the ears to hear the sighs and
sorrow of men. And that is what love looks like" (Augustine).
For a moment, love can transform the world. Leo Buscaglia
said, "Love is life . . . and if you miss love, you miss life."

*We know that we have passed from death to life
because we love one another.*

—1 JOHN 3:14 NRSV

Do all things with love. Love opens, love asks, love expands,
and love creates.

BE LIKE A TEFLON PAN: DON'T LET THINGS STICK TO YOU

I HAVE HAD THE PRIVILEGE of meeting hundreds of people over the past several years. One thing that always stands out to me is how many people have things attached to them. For example, a critical statement by a third grade teacher, a failure or mistake that they made ten or fifteen years ago, or what a noisy negative neighbor might have said last week. Not everyone has a right to speak into your life. One of the most powerful principles that we can apply to acquire momentum is *not letting things stick to us*. It is a foolish man who hears all that he hears.

I really believe that one of the major benefits of asking forgiveness from God is that things no longer retain their hold on us. He says that if we confess our sins, He is faithful and just to forgive us of our sins. Incredibly, though, God doesn't stop there (and that would be great enough); He also promises to cleanse us from all unrighteousness. When He cleanses us from all unrighteousness, we have a right standing before the Father. Why? He doesn't want things to stick to us. When we have received a right standing before the Father, we are free of the failures and mistakes, wrong words and attitudes of the past, and are released and free to accomplish things for the future.

Don't worry if you don't get what you think you should. What seems so necessary today might not even be desirable tomorrow.

In times like these, it helps to recall that there have always been times like these.

—PAUL HARVEY

If we could forget our troubles as easily as we forget our blessings, how different things would be!

One way to be free of unwanted baggage is to take your mind off the things that seem to be against you. Thinking about these negative factors simply builds them into a power that they truly don't possess. Incessantly talking about your grievances merely adds to those grievances. Attach yourself to God's forgiveness, plan, and Word ... then watch yourself become loosed from former "sticky" situations.

When God Is Number One, Everything Else Adds Up

THERE'S A FAMOUS OLD STORY about a man who was sleeping at night in his cabin when suddenly his room filled with light, and God appeared. The Lord told the man He had work for him to do, and showed him a large rock in front of the cabin. The Lord explained that the man was to push against the rock with all his might. So the man did, day after day.

For many years he toiled from sunup to sundown, his shoulders set squarely against the cold, massive surface of the unmoving rock, pushing with all of his might. Each night the man returned to his cabin sore and worn-out, feeling that his whole day had been spent in vain.

Since the man was showing discouragement, the adversary (Satan) decided to enter the picture by placing thoughts into his weary mind: "You've been pushing against that rock for a long time, and it hasn't moved." Thus, He gave the man the impression that the task was impossible and that he was a failure. These thoughts discouraged and disheartened the man. Satan said, "Why kill yourself over this? Just put in your time, giving just the minimum effort; that will be good enough."

That's what the fatigued man planned to do, but he still decided to make it a matter of prayer and take his troubled thoughts to God. "Lord," he said, "I've labored long and hard in your service, putting all my strength to do what you have asked. Yet after all this time, I have not even budged that rock by half a millimeter. What's wrong? Why am I failing?"

The Lord responded compassionately, "My friend, when I asked you to serve Me and you accepted, I told you that your task was to push against the rock with all of your strength, which you have done. Never once did I mention to you that I expected you to move it. Your task was to push.

"And now you come to Me with your strength spent, thinking that you have failed. But is that really so? Look at yourself. Your arms are strong and muscled, your back sinewy and brown; your hands are callused from constant pressure, your legs have become massive and hard. Through opposition you have grown much, and your abilities now surpass that which you used to have. True, you haven't moved the rock. But your calling was to be obedient and to push and to exercise your faith and trust in My wisdom. That you have done. Now I, my friend, will move the rock."

When God gives you a word, don't make a paragraph out of it. Usually our additions to what He says get us in trouble or cause delays. Yes, use the faith that moves mountains, but remember, it's He who will actually do it.

Many people believe *in* God, but not many believe God. One of the most incredible states in which we can live our lives is in a continual position of trusting faith:

God made us, and God is able to empower us to do whatever He calls us to do. Denying that we can accomplish God's work is not humility; it is the worst kind of pride.

—WARREN WIERSBE

The man who puts God first will find God with him right up to the last. "In everything you do, put God first, and He will direct you and crown your efforts with success" (Proverbs 3:6 TLB). Unless it includes believing God, it is not worthy of being called God's direction; every divine direction that we receive from God will include our believing Him.

> *God never made a promise that was too good to be true.*
>
> —D. L. MOODY

One of the great things about believing God is found in Luke 18:27: "The things which are impossible with men are possible with God." When you join together with Him in His plan, things that were impossible become possible. What the superior man seeks is in God. What the small man seeks is in himself or in others. You have not tapped God's resources until you have attempted the impossible.

You may trust the Lord too little, but you can never trust Him too much. With God's strength behind you, His love within you, and His arms beneath you, you are more than sufficient for the days ahead of you.

> *I trust that God is on our side. But it is more important to know that we are on God's side.*
>
> —ABRAHAM LINCOLN

The fact is that anyone who doesn't believe in miracles is not a realist. Look around—nothing is more real than miracles. When you leave God out, you'll find yourself without any invisible means of support. Nothing great has ever been achieved except by those who dared to believe that God inside them was superior to circumstance.

Saying "impossible" always puts you on the losing side. If you dream big, believe big, and pray big, big things will happen. Most of the things that were worth doing in history had been declared impossible before they were done. What is "impossible" is our highest responsibility.

Stop every day and look at the size of God. The way each day appears to you starts with who or what you're looking to. Look to God. Believe God. When you trust in God, you will see an opportunity in every problem, not problems in the middle of every opportunity. Proverbs 16:3 says,

> *Commit to the* LORD *whatever you do, and your plans will succeed.*

Joshua 1:9 (TLB) says,

> *Yes, be bold and strong! Banish fear and doubt! For remember, the Lord your God is with you wherever you go.*

It's been my observation and experience that nothing humanistic works out that well. All great things have God at the center of them. Dare to go with God farther than you can see. If something is beneficial for you, God will put it within your reach:

> *No good thing will He withhold from them that walk uprightly.*
>
> —PSALM 84:11 KJV

Never undertake anything for which you wouldn't have the conviction to ask the blessing of heaven. A small man stands on others. A great man stands on God.

SOMETIMES THE MORE YOU DO, THE LESS YOU GET DONE

ONE OF THE DEVIL'S PRIMARY STRATEGIES to hinder our momentum is to use distractions to keep us from being focused on the plan that God has for us. What we should do is determine what we really want and what God wants for us. This will keep you from chasing butterflies and put you to work digging for diamonds.

Concentrate on one thing at a time, and rule out all outside influences that don't have any real bearing on the task at hand. By doing that, you'll bring your entire mind and faculties to bear, without distraction, on the problem or subject that needs your attention.

> *People are always blaming their circumstances for what they are. I don't believe in circumstances. The people who get on in this world are the people who get up and look for circumstances they want, and, if they can't find them, make them.*
>
> —GEORGE BERNARD SHAW

Within your concentration the rest of the world cannot

distract you: "Look straight ahead; don't even turn your head to look. Watch your step. Stick to the path and be safe" (Proverbs 4:25–26 TLB).

Pay more attention to the things that are working positively in your life than to those that are giving you trouble. Too many times people devote the majority of their resources to things that are never going to be productive in their lives. Clear your mind of what's out of your control in order to focus on and act upon your goals for the day.

> *If a man could have half his wishes, he would double his troubles.*
>
> —BENJAMIN FRANKLIN

You'll always get lost by trying to find an alternate route for the straight and narrow. "He will keep in perfect peace all those who trust in him, whose thoughts turn often to the Lord!" (Isaiah 26:3 TLB).

> *Life's greatest tragedy is to lose God and not miss Him.*
>
> —F. W. NORWOOD

Do just once what others say you can't do, and you will never pay attention to their limitations again. Remember, what others say will be one of the primary distractions that will try to hinder you. When you allow yourself to be distracted and disheartened by the fear and doubt that others bring to your life, you will have quick ears for bad news, have large eyes for trouble ahead, and be a great inventor of things that will never happen. Jesus said, "Anyone who lets himself be distracted from the work I plan for him is not fit for the Kingdom of God" (Luke 9:62 TLB). Keep your eyes on what's true—don't let the urgent take you from the important.

You Can Succeed Best and Quickest by Helping Others Succeed

A FEW YEARS AGO at the Special Olympics in Seattle, nine disabled contestants, all physically or mentally challenged, assembled at the starting line for the one-hundred-yard dash. At the gun, they all took off—not exactly in a dash, but with relish to finish the race and win.

All, that is, except one boy who stumbled on the asphalt, tumbled over a couple of times, and began to cry. The eight other runners heard him. They slowed down and paused. Then they all turned around and went back. *Every one of them*. One girl with Down's syndrome bent, kissed him, and said, "This will make it better." Then all nine linked arms and walked together to the finish line.

Everyone in the stadium stood, and the cheering went on for ten minutes.

Life can be unthinkably cruel and lonely if you try to do it all by yourself!

Life is a lot like tennis: Those who don't serve well end up losing. Again, we make a living by what we get; we make a life by what we give. Once more, take in these words from Peter Marshall: "The measure of life is not in its duration, but in its donation. Everyone can be great because everyone can serve." When you are serving others, life is not meaningless.

"Never forget to be truthful and kind. Hold these virtues tightly. Write them deep within your heart" (Proverbs 3:3–4 TLB). Tom Haggai says, "A self-centered life is totally empty, while an empty life allows room for God." Remember: If you are dissatisfied with your lot in life, build a service station on it. A good way to forget your troubles is to help others out of theirs.

And, as noted, serving others is never entirely unselfish, for the giver never fails to receive: "Your own soul is nourished when you are kind; it is destroyed when you are cruel" (Proverbs 11:17 TLB). Self-interest is a fire that consumes others and then self. Since nine-tenths of our unhappiness is selfishness, think instead in terms of what someone else wants. It is literally true that you can succeed best and quickest by helping others succeed.

A true servant helps other people become motivated by guiding them to their gifts, callings, talents, and strengths. The true purpose of a leader is to help others get from where they are to where they haven't yet been. We increase whatever we praise, and the deepest need in human nature is the need to be appreciated and loved.

Few things in the world are more powerful than a positive push. A smile. A word of optimism and hope. A "you can do it" when things are tough.
—RICHARD DE VOS

Look for ways to help others by praising them. From now on, any definition of a successful life must include serving others.

POSITION YOURSELF TO RECEIVE, NOT RESIST

A ONE-DOLLAR BILL MET a twenty-dollar bill and said, "Hey, where've you been? I haven't seen you around here much."

The twenty answered, "I've been hanging out at the casinos, went on a cruise and did the rounds of the ship, back to the United States for a while, went to a couple of baseball games, to the mall, that kind of stuff. How about you?"

The one said, "You know, same old stuff—church, church, church."

How you position yourself to receive makes all the difference. For example, as you read this book, if you position yourself to receive by saying to the Lord, *I will take action on what you show me,* you will benefit more than if you read it just to be motivated or inspired. Action springs not from thought but from a readiness for responsibility. Position yourself to be ready for responsibility.

I've known many people who were excellent reservoirs of learning yet never had a new idea.

Eyes that look are common. Eyes that see are rare.
—J. OSWALD SANDERS

The problem is, we're flooded with information and starving for revelation.

To resist or receive is a choice we make every day, sometimes on many occasions each day. Nothing dies quicker than a new idea in a closed mind. It is impossible for a man to learn what he thinks he already knows. I believe one of the reasons Jesus responded so strongly to the Pharisees was because they refused to position themselves to receive.

Availability is the greatest ability you have. The devil trembles when he hears God's weakest servant say, "Yes, Lord." When you're facing God, your back is turned to the devil. Never give up control of your life to anything but faith.

Our walk with God begins with the word *follow* and ends with the word *go*! The devil shakes when he hears us say, *I'll do as you say, Lord.*

Kneeling is the proper posture for putting seeds into the ground.

—BROOKS ATKINSON

The Christian on his knees sees more than the world on its tiptoes.

The main problem is that we won't let God help us. Never be so poor that you cannot afford to pay attention.

By how we position ourselves, we can see the evidence of God everywhere, or nowhere. Does God seem far away? Guess who moved! "I spake unto thee in thy prosperity, but thou saidst, I will not hear" (Jeremiah 22:21 KJV). It will be a great thing for the human soul when it finally stops worshiping backward.

"Many Nobel prizes have been washed down the drain because someone did not expect the unexpected," said Dietrich Bonhoeffer. A wrongly positioned mind is like a microscope, which magnifies trifling things but cannot receive great ones. Every situation, properly viewed, is an opportunity.

You will never see the sun rise by looking to the west. Opportunities can drop in your lap if you have your lap where opportunities drop. When you don't position yourself to receive, it's like asking for a bushel while carrying a cup. Don't pray for rain if you're going to complain about the mud.

We typically see things not as they are but as we are. Too often our minds are locked on one track. We are looking for red, so we overlook blue; we are thinking tomorrow, and God is saying *now;* we are looking everywhere, and the answer is right under our nose.

When a person is positioned correctly, he is ready to receive all that God has for him.

GOD REJOICES OVER YOU

ONE SUNDAY MORNING the congregation of a ritzy church (with vaulted ceilings, hand-carved oak pews, stained-glass windows, and deep plush carpet) had a stir. A man came in just minutes before the service was to begin; he was dressed horribly, in boots, dirty overalls, a flannel shirt, and a cowboy hat.

The congregation was aghast, buzzing with concern. At the end of the service the minister greeted the humbly dressed man and asked him if he enjoyed the service. The man said that he enjoyed it very much. The minister then asked the man to consider dressing differently, and told him to pray to Jesus about how He would have him dress if he came back to the church the following Sunday.

The next week the man returned. He was dressed the same, and once again the congregation was disturbed. At the end of the service, the minister greeted the man and asked him what Jesus had said concerning his "church attire." The man replied, "I spoke with Jesus about this, but He said He didn't know how I should dress for this church, because He's never been here before."

It's not how you dress your body, it's how you dress your heart.

You are not insignificant. Never view your life as if Jesus did nothing for you. Make the most of yourself, for that is all God made of you. The first and worst of all frauds is the betrayal of yourself. If you deliberately plan to be less than you are capable of being, you will bring unhappiness to the rest of your life.

Too many people never begin to do what God wants them to do because they are waiting to be able to sing like Sandi Patti, preach like Billy Graham, or write like Chuck Swindoll before they begin. God knew what He was doing when He put you together. Use the talents you possess. The woods would be very silent if the only birds that made any sound were those that sang the very best.

You were created for achievement. You have been given the seeds for greatness. What is greatness? What is achievement? *Doing what God wants you to do and being where He wants you to be.*

Christians are new creations, not rebuilt sinners. Don't ever forget that God calls you friend (see John 15:15). What an incredible statement that is! He also says you are "wonderfully made" (see Psalm 139:14).

You're beginning to see that God made you special for a purpose. He has a job for you that no one else can do as well as you. Out of the billions of applicants, only one is qualified, only one has the right combination of what it takes. God has given each person the measure of faith to do what He has called him to do. Every person is gifted.

A person is never what he ought to be until he is doing what he ought to be doing. God holds us responsible not for what we have but for what we could have, not for what we are but for what we might be. We are responsible to God for becoming what God has made possible for us to become.

Your life makes a difference. There are no unimportant people. Although we're all different, no mixture is insignificant.

On Judgment Day, God won't ask me why I wasn't King David or George Bush but why I wasn't John Mason. Jerry Van Dyke said it well:

The best rose bush is not the one with the fewest thorns, but that which bears the finest roses.

EVERY SUCCESSFUL PERSON IS BEING HELPED BY SOMEONE ELSE

CHARLES PLUM, A U.S. Naval Academy graduate, was a jet pilot in Vietnam. After seventy-five combat missions, his plane was destroyed by a surface-to-air missile. Plum ejected, parachuted into enemy hands, and was captured, spending six years in a communist prison. He survived the ordeal and now lectures on lessons learned from that experience.

One day when he and his wife were sitting in a restaurant, a man from another table came up and said, "You're Plum! You flew jet fighters in Vietnam from the aircraft carrier *Kitty Hawk*. You were shot down!"

"How in the world did you know that?" asked Plum.

"I packed your parachute," the man replied.

Plum gasped in surprise and gratitude. The man grabbed his hand and said, "I guess it worked!"

Plum assured him, "It sure did. If your chute hadn't worked, I wouldn't be here today."

Plum couldn't sleep that night, thinking about that man. He kept wondering what the man might have looked like in a Navy uniform. He wondered how many times he might have seen him and not even said "Good morning" or "How are you" or anything else, because, you see, he was a fighter pilot; the other man was just a sailor. Plum thought of the many hours that sailor had spent in the bowels of the ship, carefully weaving the shrouds and folding the silks of each chute, holding in his hands the fate of someone he didn't know.

Now Plum asks his audience, "Who's packing your parachute?" Everyone has someone who provides what he needs to make it through the day.

No one makes it alone. Have a grateful heart and be quick to acknowledge those who help you. The fence that shuts others out, shuts you in. There is no such thing as a "self-made man"; we're all made up of thousands of others. The man who only works by himself and for himself is likely to be corrupted by the company he keeps. George Adams says, "Everyone who has ever done a kind deed for us, or spoken one word of encouragement to us, has entered into the makeup of our character and of our thoughts, as well as our success."

> *I not only use all the brains I have, but all that I can borrow.*
>
> —WOODROW WILSON

Make yourself indispensable to somebody.

If you blame others for your failures, do you credit others with your successes? Behind a capable person there are always other capable people. Work with others. Remember the banana: every time it leaves the bunch, it gets peeled and eaten. You'll never experience lasting success without solid relationships. No one alone can match the cooperative effort of the right team.

> *Tunnel vision tells you nobody is working as hard as you are. Tunnel vision is an enemy of teamwork. Tunnel vision is a door through which division and strife enter.*
>
> —TIM REDMOND

Few burdens are heavy when everybody lifts. Even freckles would make a nice coat of tan if they would get together.

The man who believes in nothing but himself lives in a very small world. The man who sings his own praises may have the right tune but the wrong words. The higher you go in life, the more dependent you will become on other people. A conceited person never gets anywhere because he thinks he is already there. Every great man is always being helped by somebody else.

FAITH IS LIKE A TOOTHBRUSH: USE IT DAILY, BUT DON'T USE SOMEONE ELSE'S

G O FROM BEING DEPENDENT on others to being dependent on God. He is the source of our direction. Too many people base what they believe, do, and say on what other people believe, do, and say; revelation is only revelation when it's your revelation. God is best known by revelation, not explanation. This is what Jesus meant in Matthew 16:16–17 when He said, in response to Peter's comment, "You are the Christ, the Son of the living God. . . . This was not revealed to you by man, but by my Father in heaven."

Our faith works only when we believe it and place a demand on it. If another person's faith can't get you to heaven, it can't get you to your earthly destiny either. The devil can't give us anything without bankrupting us of something else, but God can't give us anything without blessing everything else.

There are two kinds of unwise people. One says, "This is old, therefore it is good." The other says, "This is new, therefore it is better." Do not attempt to do something unless you are sure of it yourself; however, do not abandon it simply because someone else is not sure of you.

God uses others to speak to us. Ministers, books, tapes, music, and television are all ways He might use to reach us and teach us. But don't believe something just because Brother So-and-So believes it. Believe because God has shown it to you and confirmed it in His Word. The most important convictions in our lives cannot be reached on the word of another. The fact is,

> *The Bible is so simple you have to have someone else help you misunderstand it.*
>
> —CHARLES CAPPS

God desires a personal relationship with you. People who don't pray and discover the truth for themselves are really declaring that they don't need God. Judas heard all of Christ's sermons, but obviously he didn't allow them to become personal revelation. John Wesley said it well:

> *When I was young I was sure of everything; in a few years, having been mistaken a thousand times, I was not half so sure of most things as I was before; at present, I am hardly sure of anything but what God has revealed to me.*

You'll always be more convinced by what you've discovered than by what others have found.

At the End of Life, No One Says He Wishes He'd Spent More Time at the Office

THE AMERICAN INVESTMENT BANKER was at the pier of a small Mexican coastal village when a small boat with just one fisherman docked. Inside the boat were several large yellowfin tuna. The banker complimented the Mexican on the quality of his fish and asked how long it took to catch them.

The fisherman replied, "Only a little while."

The banker then asked, "Why didn't you stay out longer and catch more fish?"

The fisherman said, "With this I have more than enough to support my family's needs."

The banker pressed, "But what do you do with the rest of your time?"

The fisherman answered, "I sleep late, fish a little, play with my children, take siesta with my wife, Maria, stroll into the village each evening where I sip wine and play guitar with my amigos ... I have a full and busy life."

The banker scoffed. "I'm a Harvard MBA and could help

you. You should spend more time fishing; with the proceeds, buy a bigger boat. With the proceeds from the bigger boat, you could buy several boats. Eventually you would have a fleet of fishing boats. Instead of selling your catch to a middleman, you would sell directly to the processor, eventually opening your own cannery. You would control the product, processing, and distribution. You'd leave this little village and move to Mexico City, then Los Angeles, and eventually New York, where you'd run your ever-expanding enterprise."

The fisherman asked, "But how long will this all take?"

The banker replied, "Fifteen to twenty years."

"What then?" asked the fisherman.

The banker laughed. "That's the best part. When the time is right, you would announce an IPO, sell your company stock to the public, and become very rich; you'd make millions."

"Millions? . . . Then what?"

"Then you would retire. Move to a small coastal fishing village, where you would sleep late, fish a little, play with your kids, take siesta with your wife, stroll to the village in the evenings, where you could sip wine and play your guitar with your amigos" (Author unknown).

> *Jesus never taught men how to make a living. He taught men how to live. God doesn't call us to be successful. He calls us to be faithful.*
>
> —ALBERT HUBBARD

Most people have their eye on the wrong goal. Is more money, a higher position, or more influence your goal? These are not goals; they are the by-products of true goals.

What is a true goal?

Do not let this Book of the Law depart from your mouth; meditate on it day and night, so that you may be careful to do everything written in it. Then you will be prosperous and successful. (Joshua 1:8)

Seek not success, but seek the truth, and you will find both. We should work to become, not to acquire. Measure wealth not by the things you have but by the things you have for which you would not take money.

> *Happiness is not a reward—it is a consequence. Suffering is not a punishment—it is a result.*
>
> —ROBERT GREEN INGERSOLL

Success lies not in achieving what you aim at but in aiming at what you ought to achieve. Rate the path higher than the prize. Do the very best you can, and leave the results to God.